Creating Opportunities for Change and Organization Development in Southern Africa

A volume in
Contemporary Trends in Organization Development
Peter F. Sorensen and Therese Yaeger, *Series Editors*

Creating Opportunities for Change and Organization Development in Southern Africa

Dalitso Samson Sulamoyo

Illinois Association of Community Action Agencies

IAP

INFORMATION AGE PUBLISHING, INC.

Charlotte, NC • www.infoagepub.com

Library of Congress Cataloging-in-Publication Data

Sulamoyo, Dalitso Samson.
Creating opportunities for change and organization development in Southern Africa / Dalitso Samson Sulamoyo.
p. cm. – (Contemporary trends in organization development)
Includes bibliographical references.
ISBN 978-1-62396-031-5 (pbk.) – ISBN 978-1-62396-032-2 (hbk.) – ISBN 978-1-62396-033-9 (ebook) 1. Organizational behavior–Africa, Southern. 2. Organizational change–Africa, Southern. 3. Management–Africa, Southern. I. Title.
HD58.7.S923 2012
658.4'060968–dc23

2012033285

Printed and bound by CPI Group (UK) Ltd, Croydon, CR0 4YY

Contents

Foreword

We are proud to present this seventh book in our Contemporary Trends in OD series. This book, *Global and International Organization Development: Creating Opportunities for Change and Development in Southern Africa,* by Dr. Dalitso Sulamoyo, clearly provides us with essential information on one of the most important trends for the field, now and even more so for the future; namely, Organization Development on the continent of Africa.

The timeliness of this book could not be more appropriate. A recent publication by the McKinsey Global Institute (2010) indicates that the growth for Africa is unprecedented, stating,

> Africa's collective economy grew very little during the last two decades of the 20th century. But sometime in the late 1990s, the continent began to stir. GDP growth picked up and then bounded ahead, rising faster and faster through 2008. Today, while Asia's tiger economies continue to expand rapidly, we foresee the potential rise of economic lions in Africa's future.

Similarly, we aptly see Dr. Dalitso Sulamoyo, with his work on OD in Africa, as the "scholar on the move" as he provides this unfolding and important contribution to the field of Organization Development. Dalitso provides us with a number of insights, including the depth and breadth of OD in sub-Sahara Africa, the kinds of interventions employed, the role of indigenous OD, and the application of African concepts to work here in the United States. This author presents us with a truly remarkable piece of work. It is our hope that this book is but the first of a number of pub-

Creating Opportunities for Change and OD in Southern Africa, pages ix–x

lications by the author, each new publication building on previous work; each one providing increased understanding of this very important trend in global OD.

—Peter F. Sorensen, PhD
Therese F. Yaeger, PhD
Benedictine University

Reference

McKinsey Global Institute. (2010). Lions on the move: The progress and potential of African economies. *McKinsey Global Institute.* Retrieved from http://www.mckinsey.com/Insights/MGI/Research/Productivity_Competitiveness_and_Growth/Lions_on_the_move

Preface

When I moved to the United States 20 years ago, I was greatly surprised at how little people knew about Africa and about my small country of Malawi. Most astounding was the fact that many considered Africa one big country with a monolithic culture, a single language, and never-ending civil wars, disease, famine, and wildlife. Their knowledge of Africa was imbued with many negative and pessimistic connotations. They were not aware of the existence of metropolitan areas in the countries of Africa. Most were oblivious to the fact that the rich history of great African civilizations has left an indelible mark on the foundation of modern history. This pessimistic view was not limited to people from other parts of the world. I have found that many Africans perpetuate this pessimistic view when they talk about their own countries. It is not unusual to hear descriptions of countries begin with poverty statistics, the impact of the HIV/AIDS pandemic, or discussions of political instability. Although this approach may be used to invoke sympathy from an audience, it perhaps limits the opportunities for change and development because the pessimism can be overwhelming.

Some 20 years later, I have found that Africa is still an enigma to the West, a status perpetuated by its paradoxes. The continent of Africa is wealthy in resources; however, its people are the most impoverished in the world. Africa is multidimensional in terms of its social, political, economic, and cultural attributes. Having been born to parents from two different countries, I have an appreciation for the multicultural settings found in African countries. Many times these differences are portrayed in the West

Creating Opportunities for Change and OD in Southern Africa, pages xi–xviii as contributing factors to Africa's problems. On the contrary, I have found that the multicultural differences are what make the continent of Africa culturally wealthy.

After having lived in America for over 20 years, it can be assumed that I have assimilated well into the American or Midwestern culture. I would argue that part of my assimilation has involved the sharing of my culture. I have had the opportunity to share the culture of *Ubuntu* or *Umuthu* in my professional career. Ubuntu, as it is discussed in this book, represents the collectivist cultural view that is prevalent in southern African cultures. As the president and CEO of a nongovernmental organization (NGO) based in the United States, I have used Ubuntu to set the tone for my organization in the last 12 years. Because we spend so much of our time at work, I have tried to build a cultural environment that is family oriented. It is not unusual for us to have employees' children running around our offices. Employees are allowed to bring their children to work if they encounter daycare complications or school closings. They also have the flexibility to work from home if their children are sick. I have found that this approach enhances performance.

The last couple of years have been financially challenging for most NGOs that rely on government funding in the United States. Congress and the president have had to make tough decisions cutting domestic programs to balance the budget and to reduce the federal deficit. Because of these financial challenges, organizations, such as the one I lead, have had to make tough decisions in laying off staff and cutting services. My approach to budget cuts has always been influenced by Ubuntu. When my organization faced cuts with some of its grants, our approach was to share the burden of the cuts organizationally. It would have been easier or perhaps made good business sense for me to lay off the staff affected by the grants that were cut; however, instead, we absorbed the cuts with other grants that were not cut. We decided to prioritize the welfare of our staff. The staff members of the organization are like a family. Our approach in this sense was the Ubuntu approach. We faced the challenges as an organization but most importantly, as a work family unit. What affected others affected us all.

South Africa hosted the 2010 World Cup soccer tournament 16 years after racial democracy was achieved in that country. Even though South Africa was the main host, the entire continent of Africa was full of pride and jubilation at the opportunity of hosting the world's largest sport on African soil. Given the negativity and pessimism that has dominated the discussions about Africa, many people were doubtful that hosting an event of such magnitude and stature could be pulled off by the South Africans and the continent of Africa. Some of the doubts were leveled at the capacity of South

Africa to host such an event because the country was still in transition from Apartheid. I am quite sure that some of the doubts were based on whether or not effective systems, structure, leadership, and organization could be matched up with the needs of such an event. It was with great pride that the world witnessed, throughout the month of the World Cup matches and activities, an event that was superbly organized and graciously hosted by South Africa. It was a proud moment for the entire continent of Africa. Such successes need to be highlighted and built upon to overcome African pessimism. This book takes a positive and strength-focused approach to the opportunities that the continent of Africa, particularly the southern part, has to offer to the field of organization development (OD).

As I was completing this book, the president of Malawi, Bingu wa Mutharika, died suddenly on April 5, 2012. The Malawian government, led by the president's party— the Democratic People's Party—decided to keep his death a secret from the Malawian people until the matter of succession was resolved. Even though Malawi had a vice president who was duly elected by the Malawian people, she had been expelled from the president's party for refusing to endorse his brother as the next presidential candidate. She consequently formed her own party, the People's Party. The constitution was clear in prescribing that in the event the president is incapacitated or dead, the vice president assumes or ascends to the presidency. What a few people in the Malawian government tried to do was subvert the constitution by politicizing the issue of succession. They took the position that because the then–vice president had formed her own party, she was not eligible to be president because she was no longer a member of the party that had won the executive branch. It took 2 days for the government to officially announce that the president had succumbed to cardiac arrest. The military, police, senior government officials, civil society organizations, and the international community took the position to let the provisions of the constitution prevail. The vice president was thus sworn in as the new president 2 days after the president died. She became the second female president in Africa. What is important here is the fact that democratic transitions can occur in Africa peacefully. This in itself should be lauded as a success story. Perhaps the autocratic political culture discussed in this book is changing in Malawi.

Many books published on management and OD over the years are featured and highlighted at various management conferences in the United States. You find books by Peter Senge, Peter Block, Peter Drucker, Warren Benis, Gert Hofstede, Henry Mintzberg, Chris Argyris, John Kotter, and many others who are household names in the field of management. These are also household names in African schools of management and have played an influential role on the continent. What is concerning is that few African scholars in the field of management are prominently featured in the West. In fact, when one searches for top management thinkers or gurus, the list is replete with mostly Western thinkers and practitioners, with some from Japan. This book recognizes some of the renowned scholars and practitioners from Africa who have approached change and management from an African perspective. Their work is not only applicable in Africa, but it can be modified to fit the Western context.

Even though I have not lived in Malawi for over 20 years, I have always believed that Africa in general has many great things to offer the world. Some of Africa's attributes can benefit the field of management and particularly, organization development. To generalize, Africa is indeed an injustice based on the richness of the continent's diversity. However, to cover every country and culture in Africa for purposes of defining management practices or approaches to OD would be a lifelong quest. This book discusses opportunities that exist for OD to make a significant impact in southern Africa. The book also reveals those opportunities to African scholars and practitioners committed to an agenda for change and development not only within organizational settings but also, more importantly, within large systems that can set new directions for Africa's countries. Finally, this book recognizes the importance of African culture, customs, and beliefs in advancing the field of management and OD.

The first objective of this book is to define *indigenized OD* within the context of global OD. *Indigenization* is the convergence of OD interventions developed in the West with local African culture, economic conditions as well as political and social conditions for success and sustainability. The movement toward indigenization should become part of an African Renaissance as defined within the context of OD and change. I have purposely chosen to utilize the *indigenization* definition, as opposed to *global OD,* because of its immediate recognition of local culture and local settings. *Indigenization* is also preferred because of its connotation of empowering African managers and OD practitioners to deliberately converge OD with their local settings. Further, within the indigenization framework is the recognition of indigenously developed applications, which also need to be accepted as legitimate practices within the framework of management and change in Africa.

The second objective of the book is to contribute knowledge to the limited literature on OD in Africa, particularly sub-Saharan Africa. This book aims to serve as the antithesis to African pessimism, which has focused on the negative aspects of the continent of Africa and not enough on the successes in management, development, and change. The book thus documents successful OD projects carried out by OD practitioners in Malawi through a collection of case studies over a 25-year period. This work is infused with African values, traditions, customs, proverbs, and metaphors. The work of practitioners such as Chiku Malunga is opening the door to Africa's indigenous efforts to affect OD and management systems within organizations.

The book uses three methods for conveying the opportunities and experience of OD in Africa: research, practitioner point of view, and storytelling. This book highlights some of the scholarly work by Africans. Their work may not have had much exposure in the West, however, their contributions to the field of management should be recognized. The time is right for change and development in southern Africa with OD as the driving force.

The first chapter defines OD and its evolutionary development as a field. The first half of this chapter is focused on the discussion of Western philosophers and theorists who provided the foundation of the field's development. It is also in this chapter where the stems or phases of OD's development are discussed. In the second half of the chapter, the introduction of OD to southern Africa is discussed. The chapter explores the conditions that have led to the field's introduction in southern Africa. The chapter concludes with the recognition of African scholars and practitioners who have approached their work and research from the African perspective and conditions. There are perhaps others who have done so but who were not mentioned in this chapter. Those who made the list particularly influenced my thinking in writing this book. Finally, some of the local OD practitioners are recognized in order to provide opportunities for partnership to those global OD practitioners who have an interest in working in that region of Africa. These local OD practitioners could prove to be invaluable for cultural translation of OD approaches that are Western developed. They could also educate global OD practitioners in indigenous practices that can be culturally translated for Western practical usage.

The second chapter defines culture and its importance within the African context. This chapter discusses the diversity of culture in Africa to refute some of its stereotyping as monolithic in the African setting. In this chapter, culture is defined through leadership models, political systems, belief systems, and the usage of proverbs and metaphors. The concept of indigenization is introduced in this chapter. This concept is preferred because of its immediate recognition of African thought in the modification of Western developed concepts to fit African settings. The concept also allows locally developed concepts to be viewed and accepted in a mainstream thought of management. The chapter embraces Terrence Jackson's idealistic "African Renaissance" concept as an antithesis to African pessimism.

This concept is aligned with the values of OD, which are optimistic, humanistic, and democratic.

The third chapter focuses on the practical applications of OD interventions in southern Africa. Case studies are utilized to demonstrate the practicality of OD interventions in southern Africa. The chapter discusses the importance of cultural translation of Western development concepts for their applicability and acceptability. Finally, this chapter introduces the P8 Planning Process, a model that utilizes proverbs from different parts of the world as a basis for reflection in defining the different stages of the planning process. This model is influenced by Chiku Malunga's (2009) strategic planning approach, which uses African proverbs for reflective thinking.

The fourth chapter discusses models that have been developed to understand and interpret cultural values and frameworks. The chapter discusses the applicability of Hofstede's cultural model as well as some of its criticisms. Some of the discussion of Hofstede's model is done from the perspective of practitioners who have applied it in their work. Alternative models are offered, particularly for the southern African setting. Binet's (1970) cultural model, which was developed by studying African ethnic groups as opposed to a multinational organization, is offered as an alternative to Hofstede's model. The Ubuntu philosophy, which is predominantly found in southern Africa, is offered as a cultural integrator for OD. Ubuntu's collective approach to society is discussed within the context of strategic OD. There is a side-by-side comparison of the three models discussed in this chapter.

The fifth chapter takes an academic approach to measuring the success of OD interventions in Malawi. The results of a meta-analysis of OD interventions from Malawi are discussed. The results of the meta-analysis are compared to cultural models to determine if their successes or failures are predicated on cultural appropriateness. An OD consulting model is proposed for Malawi based on success rates of interventions and their prevalent use by practitioners.

The sixth and final chapter of the book discusses opportunities of OD in southern Africa. The chapter discusses opportunities for OD in large-system changes. This discussion is based on the winds of change from the "Arab Spring," which could impact countries with autocratic regimes in southern Africa. The informal economy is another opportunity explored in this chapter for OD. Since this is a large sector including many countries in southern Africa, OD is proposed as an engagement framework to improve performance within that sector. The chapter also discusses the growing presence and influence of China in southern Africa. OD could assist in facilitating effective partnerships between Chinese entities and local organizations. The chapter concludes with proposals of models for different types of interventions that would be applicable in southern Africa. These discussions focus on models in team building, leadership-team models, consulting, policy development, Appreciative Inquiry, and postconflict reconciliation.

References

Binet, J. (1970). *Psychologie Economique Africaine.* Paris, France: Payot.

Malunga, C. (2009). *Making strategic plans work: Insights from African indigenous wisdom.* London, England: Adonis & Abbey.

Acknowledgements

There are several people I need to thank who have made this book possible. First, I thank my family for their continued support and understanding. I am grateful to Drs. Peter F. Sorensen and Therese F. Yaeger for their encouragement and support. They asked me to contribute to their series on *Contemporary Trends in Organization Development and Change* by focusing on the opportunities for organization development in southern Africa. They have been patient with me as the completion date of the manuscript and publication of the book shifted from month to month.

I am grateful to my editors, Lynn Waldman and Gail Pieper, who spent many hours going through the manuscript. Finally, I would like to thank Sara Ratcliffe for designing the graphics/figures for the book.

Creating Opportunities for Change and OD in Southern Africa, page xix

1

Understanding OD

I would like to leave behind me the conviction that if we maintain a certain amount of caution and organization we deserve victory . . . You cannot carry out fundamental change without a certain amount of madness. In this case, it comes from nonconformity, the courage to turn your back on the old formulas, the courage to invent the future. It took the madmen of yesterday for us to be able to act with extreme clarity today. I want to be one of those madmen. We must dare to invent the future.

—Thomas Sankara, 1985

Organizations in Africa apply management practices that are dominated by Western frameworks infused with African cultural, social, political, economic, legal, and technological experiences. The marriage of Western and African approaches to organizational management is not always blissful, particularly when Western approaches are positioned to dominate their counterparts. The question of change, whether it is at the level of a large system or of an organization, has always been based on how that change is facilitated given the local conditions prevalent in a given setting. The African organizational experience has, to a large extent, been influenced by what may be defined as the dominant national culture. Thus, when we talk of facilitating change within organizations, we have to understand not only how those changes fit within the context of organizational culture but how they fit within the context of national culture.

Creating Opportunities for Change and OD in Southern Africa, pages 1–23

Since organization development (OD) is a field that was developed in the West, we need to understand its evolutionary development and how its transplantation has influenced the change and development of some organizations in Africa. Equally important, we need to understand how its effective transplantation can lead to successful change and development in Africa.

Evolution and Definition of Organization Development

The first section of this chapter discusses the background and evolutionary development of organization development and provides context for the overall development of the field. What is OD? What theoretical and philosophical perspectives define OD? Cummings and Worley (2005) define organization development as follows:

> Organization Development is system wide application and transfer of behavioral science and knowledge to a planned development, improvement, and reinforcement of the strategies, structures, and processes that lead to organization effectiveness. (p. 1)

OD Theorists and Philosophers

Many OD philosophers and theorists significantly influenced the development of OD as a movement before its official definition in the 1960s. Their work, particularly their theoretical underpinnings, is important because of the impact they have had in the development of OD and its evolution. Frederick Taylor is known as the father of scientific management and one of the pioneers of management consulting. Scientific management was designed to allow organizations or factories to perform efficiently and effectively by accounting for the need for cooperative roles and relationships between management and labor. Taylor defined scientific management as having five principles, "science, not rule of thumb; harmony, not discord; cooperation, not individualism; maximum output, not restricted output; and development of each man to his greatest efficiency and prosperity" (1915, p. 140). According to Weisbord (2004, p. 61), Taylorism embraces the following core values: labor-management cooperation, higher output, improved quality, lower costs, higher wages, the rule of reason, questioning old habits, experimentation, clear tasks and goals, feedback, training, mutual help and support, stress reduction, and careful selection and development of people. Organizations still embrace these values today in both management and labor. The challenge within the context of OD arises when Taylorism is applied without taking into account equity from increased productivity.

Credited as the founder of social psychology, Kurt Lewin was one of the first researchers to study group dynamics and organization development (Burke, 2006; Cummings & Worley, 2005; Mirvis, 1988). Lewin's personal history had a significant impact on his ideas and focus of study. He fled Nazi Germany, where he experienced persecution because of his Jewish faith. His experience led him to base his ideas and philosophy on the need to empower those who may not otherwise have the ability to facilitate social change. According to Gallos (2006), "Lewin was thus intensely interested in the study of autocratic versus democratic behavior and matters of influence and change" (p. 25).

Lewin had studied Taylor and was intrigued by the scientific thinking that he had pioneered in organizational management (Weisbord, 2004). However, Lewin took Taylor's model of scientific management and integrated it into his own democratic values to produce a participative approach to management. Lewin developed three models of how organizational change occurs or how one can facilitate change. OD still applies these models in various forms today. The first model is what he defined as the action research model. Essentially, this model of change allows organizations to solve their problems while they study their process for purposes of refining the theory of practice and change (Weisbord, 2004). The second model describes the process of change. In this model, Lewin argues that in order for change to begin in an organization, a presentation of information and education must occur, which leads to an "unfreezing process" or change in the status quo. This unfreezing process pushes against any resistance to change. Once this unfreezing occurs, there is "movement" toward the direction of change (Figure 1.1). The third part of the process is "refreezing," which he

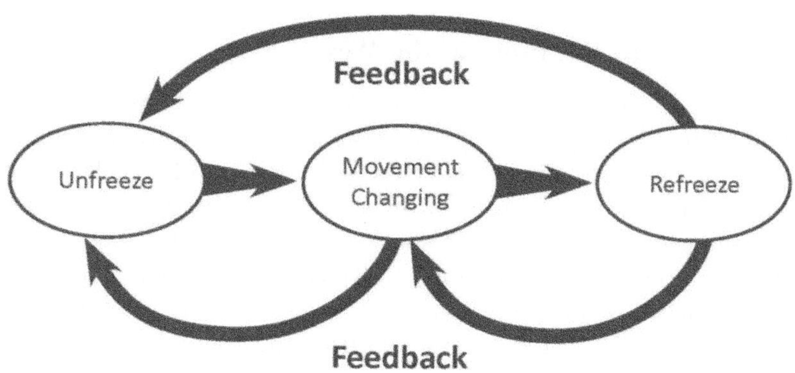

Figure 1.1 Lewin's Planned Change model.

described as a new status quo or institutionalization of change (Cummings & Worley, 2005, pp. 23–24). The third model is an assessment for change he called a force field analysis. This model is used to measure which forces are greater for change or for resistance to change against the status quo (Weisbord, 2004, p. 83).

Another organizational theorist who was a precursor to OD is Douglas McGregor, who developed the theories of human motivation known as Theory X and Theory Y. Underlying these theories are the assumptions that human beings are either lazy and abhor work, or they not only want to work but enjoy work. The way talent management is handled depends on which one of these theories managers subscribe to and how they use them to motivate their employees. McGregor's model of understanding organizations can also be applied to both Lewin and Taylor. In the case of Lewin, Theory X and Theory Y can be applied to the understanding of how change is facilitated in an organization; and, in the case of Taylor, to the understanding of the relationship between management and labor.

Burke (2006, p. 38) provides the following summary of OD theorists and their perspectives of organizational system levels: (a) individual system level—Maslow and Herzberg (individual needs), Vroom and Lawler (individual expectancies and values), Hackman and Oldham (job satisfaction), and Skinner (individual performance); (b) group system level—Lewin (norms and values), Argyris (interpersonal), and Bion (group unconsciousness); and (c) organizational system level—Likert (management style), Lawrence and Lorsch (organizational structure), and Levinson (organization as a family). These system levels help with the understanding of the complexities of organizational change, particularly with the fact that there are differing dimensions to deal with when change is involved.

Development of the Field in the West

This section of the chapter mainly uses Mirvis' (1988, 1990) evolutionary account of the development of OD as the framework to define the field. How did the environment influence the development of OD? How did society influence the direction taken by OD? Mirvis (1988) argued that to analyze the evolution of OD as a social movement in the 1960s, one has to take into account the evolution of OD as being analogous to stages in the development of people, groups, and social systems (p. 25). The key arguments that led to the definition of OD in the 1960s were grounded in both the modernist and symbolic interpretive theories of organization and environment.

The environmental contingency theory, as defined by Hatch and Cunliffe (2004), is that an organization's structure is defined by what it faces in the environment. OD was defined by a period in the 1960s that marked the commencement of a social revolution in America. That environment was defined by a country at war in Vietnam and experiencing social justice movements that addressed civil rights, voter rights, and equal opportunities and sought to bring about an American society with true and practicing egalitarian principles. The environmental influences of the 1960s clearly had an impact on how the social structure of OD had to be organized. OD had to respond to the need for facilitating human expression by creating cohesion between human needs and organizational needs.

The symbolic interpretive framework that defined OD in the 1960s was institutional theory. Hatch and Cunliffe (2004) define institutional theory within the context of organizational power, control, and conflict as "concerning the distribution of power based in institutionalized expectations (cultural resources), social norms (social resources) and regulations (political and legal resources)" (p. 256). During the 1960s, OD principles were relatively coherent and focused mainly on the social side of organizations. Since OD was based on group dynamics, many human process interventions were implemented. The best known are *t*-groups, process consultation, and team building. The emphasis was on humanistic values promoting openness, trust, and collaboration (Mirvis, 1988).

OD in the 1960s focused on creating cohesion between people and organizations through a top-down human association. According to Mirvis (1988), the birth and development of OD as a paradigm happened in three stages. The first stage dealt with a general systems theory, which initially had been limited to biological and physical phenomena but now was applied to understanding organizations. Second was the development of dynamic models of change. These models (discussed later in this chapter under the section dealing with the practice of OD) created the framework for planning and interventions. Third was the development of a model for laboratory training and consultation.

During the 1970s, OD was consolidated and formalized as a structure to address organizational effectiveness as well as inequality and discrimination in the workplace (Mirvis, 1988, p. 11). Even though significant legislation had been passed in the 1960s to address issues of inequality, this legislation did not automatically translate into the workplace or even services. A cultural shift could not be expected to immediately change an environment of inequalities and discrimination that had been in place for generations. The environment in which organizations did business during this period was still rife with the lack of diversity and fairness. The environmental contingency theory and institutional theory still influenced the development of OD during this time. According to Mirvis (1988), much of OD in the 1970s addressed employees' rights by confronting structural barriers based on race, sex, class, and organizational status. OD in 1970s thus focused on creating more diverse organizations (p. 11).

Gradually during the 1970s, new concepts emerged, influenced by organization theory and the human side of technology. Examples of this period are structural change, employee involvement, and work design. As a result, the traditional OD values favoring humanism expanded to include concerns for organizational effectiveness and bottom-line results. On the other hand, OD transitioned from theory to practice. It focused on personal and group development. In particular, OD took on its formal structure in the 1970s, promoting forms of individual and organizational behavior. OD interventions in this period helped advance human resource management and organizational effectiveness. OD also went through a formalization process in academia; management-by-objectives measured OD activities and rewarded accomplishments (Mirvis, 1988, pp. 12–13).

Business faced turbulent times in the 1980s. The recession was marked by high unemployment, high oil prices, and slow farm productivity due to a declining economy. President Reagan's domestic programs were rooted in his belief that the nation would prosper if the power of the private economic sector was unleashed. He was a proponent of "supply-side" economics, a theory that, according to Nouriel Roubini (1997), argues that lower tax rates improve private sector incentives leading to higher employment, productivity, and output in the U.S. economy. According to Mirvis (1988), Reagan's agenda in that era was to deregulate industry and privatize many social welfare functions (p. 35). Reagan "block-granted" many of the social programs to the states because he believed that the states, if empowered, would be in a better position to resolve social issues.

OD was not only impacted by the economic conditions of the 1980s but also by the responses to how those conditions were handled by the Reagan administration. With deregulation, businesses needed to be more creative and strategic. OD found its place as the vehicle that would provide the planning and strategic thinking for businesses, as the environment of the 1980s also marked the growth of OD. OD grew as an academic discipline, featured in business schools and research centers. In the 1980s, many management consultants wanted to apply OD principles because they were proving successful. Consequently, more new concepts and approaches were integrated into the current OD theory. Techniques for reward systems, career planning and development, and employee-assistance programs were developed. It was also during this period that OD became linked to human resources management within the organizational structure. The tools of organization theory and strategic management contributed to OD, along with organization design, corporate culture, strategy formulation and implementation, self-designed organizations, and transorganizational development. Production concepts were incorporated, particularly process control and quality management.

OD values are described as humanistic, optimistic, and democratic. According to French and Bell (1999), the humanistic value emphasizes the importance of individuals, the optimistic value assumes that people are essentially good, and the democratic value ensures freedom from the arbitrary misuse of power.

The goals for OD are organizational effectiveness and the improvement of the quality of life for members of human systems. Alderfer's (1997) definition of OD aligns with this statement:

> Organization Development (OD) is at once a professional field of social action and an area of academic study. The practice of organization development is aimed toward improving the quality of life for members of human systems and increasing the institutional effectiveness of those systems. The scholarly investigation of organization development seeks to understand planned change processes, to assess the effects of efforts to promote social change, and to evolve better theories of change processes. (p. 197)

These values and goals should influence the application of OD in organizations today.

The Practice of Organization Development

Cummings and Worley (2005) identify five stems of OD practice in the field: *t*-groups, action research/survey feedback, normative approaches, quality work life, and strategic change (p. 6).

Laboratory Training T-Groups

Developed by Kurt Lewin and his staff at the Massachusetts Institute of Technology, laboratory training, also known as *t*-groups, is the first stem of OD. According to Cummings and Worley (2005), Lewin had been asked by a couple of organizations that dealt with racial sensitivity issues to develop a training program or workshop for community leaders for solving problems. The workshop participants engaged in problem-solving discussions during the day, and in the evenings they discussed their observations from the perspective of group dynamics and behavior. This interaction between the researchers and the workshop participants became the basis of the *t*-group approach.

This approach to problem solving soon became integrated into business and industry and became a program of the National Training Laboratory of the National Education Association (Cummings & Worley, 2005, p. 7). The *t*-group thus became the first intervention under the formally defined field of OD. The *t*-groups were used as a tool for team building and for helping work groups become more effective. Cummings and Worley (2005) state that the *t*-group approach gradually declined as an intervention in OD because others viewed it as a "touchy-feely" method (p. 7).

Action Research/Survey Feedback

Lewin also led in the development of action research, OD's second stem. Action research is based on the premise that research should be closely linked to action if organizations are to manage change. The data collected about an organization is used to guide changes that make the organization better. The action research model continues to be the foundation of many intervention strategies applied by OD practitioners (Cummings & Worley, 2005, p. 8).

Participative Management

Participative management was developed after the first two cited stems of OD. The premise behind this approach is that organizational challenges can be resolved through human relations. According to Cummings and Worley (2005), this normative approach was developed from research done on Likert's participative management and Blake and Moulton's Grid Organization Development programs as means of bringing about organizational effectiveness (p. 9). Likert developed the following four types of management systems as characteristics for organizations: (a) exploitive authoritative systems—top-down approach; (b) benevolent authoritative systems—top-down but more paternalistic approach; (c) consultative systems—increased employee interaction and decision making; and (d) participative group systems—high degree of employee involvement and participation. Blake and Moulton, on the other hand, developed a grid to help understand leadership styles. Their quadrant grid characterizes leadership styles based on concerns for production versus concerns for people.

Quality Work Life

Quality work life is the fourth stem developed as an intervention in OD. Quality work life was developed in the United Kingdom with foundations attributed to Taylor, McGregor, and Lewin. According to Cummings and Worley (2005), quality work life involves the joint participation of labor and management in the design of work. This approach gives employees high levels of discretion, task variety, and feedback about results (pp. 10–11).

Strategic Change

The fifth and most recent stem to be developed in OD is strategic change. This stem aligns the organization's internal design with its environment (Cummings & Worley, 2005, p. 12). If an organization goes through strategic change, it should examine its structure, processes, culture, and strategy to ensure that they are aligned to withstand and effectively respond to changes, particularly if they are emanating from the external environment.

Introduction of the Field in Southern Africa

Over the past 50 years, Africa has been going through evolutionary transitions that have been political, economic, and social in nature. Politically, most African countries, except for Liberia and Ethiopia, had been colonized by European powers during the "Scramble for Africa" that took place in the late 1800s. These countries gained independence from colonial powers in the late 1950s and throughout the 1960s after liberation struggles and negotiations for independence. Most of these countries soon evolved into authoritarian regimes with one-party systems of government. The early 1990s saw the winds of change sweep these authoritarian regimes into more pluralistic forms of government. Currently, most of these countries are pseudodemocracies. Countries like Malawi and Zimbabwe hold general elections for both their legislative and their executive branches of government. Nonetheless, numerous allegations of repression and violation of human rights remain.

The history of Africa is defined by turbulent times, which have been the result of both external and internal forces. These forces have defined significant eras in the development of Africa as a paradoxical continent, wealthy in resources and yet inhabited by the most impoverished people in the world. The first era (early 1800s) is defined by the spread of religion on the African continent through Islam and Christianity. As mentioned earlier, these religions were brought to the continent of Africa with the cultures of the people who spread them. The spread of these religions affected local culture and customs, often with a clash of cultures as the invading culture attempted to either change or replace the local culture in the name of religion.

The second era (late 1800s) is defined as the "Scramble for Africa." It is a period during which European states claimed African territory to set up colonies for purposes of acquiring raw materials and minerals for their economies. This period marked the official establishment of European rule and governance on the continent of Africa. Countries like England, Portugal, Belgium, France, Spain, and Germany claimed African territories as their own. Colonial regimes were set up with systems of government modeled after the home governments. The legacy that these colonial regimes left on the continent of Africa remains indelible today as the continent strives to Africanize itself.

The third era (1960s) witnessed independence movements, as the colonies broke away from their colonial masters to become independent, self-governing states. These movements for independence were at times very violent or resulted in war to bring about the change for self-rule and governance. Postindependence was marked with transitional challenges of maintaining Eurocentric systems of governance and administration by native Africans. The struggle was defined by the need to maintain stability through mimicry of the colonizers and a hybridization of systems of government. During this third era, Africa experienced the consolidation of authoritarian regimes led by the same people who fought for independence. In spite of these major changes, the West maintained its influence on the continent through aid and the politics of the Cold War.

The fourth era (1990s) is marked by transformational winds of change, which were funneled by both internal and external pressure. Democratization became the definition of open relations with the West and the prerequisite for foreign aid. During this era, the countries selected for this study introduced multiparty democracy after decades of authoritarian regimes. This period still defines transitional challenges faced by Africa today as Africa strives to be significant in a global environment. This is the period of Africa's history when OD values, which are humanistic, optimistic, and democratic in nature, aligned with the values of change in Africa on a macro level. The replacement of authoritarian regimes with more democratic ones witnessed the emergence of regimes that promised to be more inclusive, rights enhancing, and nonoppressive (Ndegwa, 2001, p. 2).

The transitional period has been marked with the challenges of consolidating democracy while striving to survive in the world's economic arena.

The end of the Cold War in the early 1990s meant that for these predominantly pro-West countries, the lavish support they enjoyed from the West for their aligned values dissipated or came with more "strings attached."

Socially, many issues have been impacting the continent. Africa continues to deal with poverty, disease, civil conflicts, and other social issues, all of which have resulted in the proliferation of locally based, nongovernmental organizations (NGOs). The NGOs have addressed these issues when governments have failed to do so. In some respects, NGOs have become the fourth branch of government after the judicial, executive, and legislative branches. Even though they are not part of government, they provide checks and balances on the three branches of government in Africa.

Economically, Africa has for many years been working with international NGOs such as the World Bank, the International Monetary Fund, and various branches of the United Nations. These NGOs provide funding for specific initiatives and, with that funding, may require the recipient countries to engage in capacity building to ensure that the goals for the funding earmarked for specific projects and programs are accomplished. Stavros (1998) defined capacity building as "a process designed to allow an organization to attain its vision, mission and goals, and sustain itself" (p. 28). She described capacity building as involving the following:

- Participatory learning
  - Mutual learning and growth
  - Active learning
  - Collaboration
  - Learning organization
- Applied at multilevels
  - Organizational
  - Multiorganizational
  - Global
  - Nonhierarchical
- Relational connections
  - Shared objectives
  - Trust
  - Dialogue
  - Cooperation

Over the years, capacity building has been integrated with OD. The emergence of OD in southern Africa has varied, given limited opportunities for education and training in the field. For instance, in South Africa, Louw Du Toit, in partnership with American OD experts, was involved in efforts to effect large-system changes during Apartheid in the 1980s. Other countries experienced the emergence of the field of OD through the roles of international NGOs that wanted to yield more sustainable results for their efforts. According to James (2004),

> During the 1990s, OD became increasingly emphasized and supported by donors in their work with African NGOs. Yet even a cursory analysis of theories of culture and organization (see Hofstede, 1991; Trompenaars, 1993) raises fundamental questions about the relevance to Africa of this participatory, Western approach to change that relies on cultural assumptions of open discussion and individualistic, humanistic values. (p. 314)

In Malawi, the OD movement was introduced in 1998 by the International NGO Training and Research Centre (INTRAC), a not-for-profit organization based in Oxford, England. According to Watson and Collingwood (2008), INTRAC's capacity-building and OD activities in Malawi were highly successful:

> INTRAC has played a key role in establishing learning relationships between some key leaders, facilitated the emergence of two values-led OD organizations, and built a discourse around OD in Malawi—of which the analysis and documentation will be referred to as a resource for many years to come. The INTRAC Program worked with the ODPs to take on research and propose policy change to tackle the effects of HIV/AIDS which was "close to home" and a clear need—and through this way of working enabled a number of NGO leaders and program staff to develop experience and confidence in action research. All of the above examples involved linking and learning—a capacity and a value which remains within Malawi and is a building block for future strategies to develop the sector and improved development practice. (p. 5)

Watson and Collingwood (2008) state that INTRAC's approach to capacity building and introduction of OD involved a seven-pronged approach. The first approach involved the intensive training of select college graduates into becoming OD practitioners. These OD practitioners then partnered with their trainer, Rick James of INTRAC, to facilitate OD interventions that involved strategic planning, leadership coaching, team building, and governance support of NGO boards. The third approach involved leadership development: INTRAC developed a leadership training program for NGOs. The fourth approach involved research and publications: INTRAC researched and published articles on OD and the capacity building of NGOs and civil society organizations in Malawi. The fifth approach involved policy research and advocacy: INTRAC facilitated the collaboration of the OD practitioners and NGOs to research and advocate on major policy issues in Malawi such as HIV/AIDS and poverty reduction strategies. The sixth approach involved the establishment of regional networking opportunities between INTRAC and other African OD organizations to share lessons learned. The seventh approach involved establishment by INTRAC of a program that linked research and the practice of OD.

African Theorists and Practitioners

This section of the chapter discusses the work of some of the notable scholars of African management. Many of these scholars have received limited or no attention in the West. However, these scholars were selected because of their positions for viewing the field of management and OD from the perspective of their African setting. Abstracts from their published work are presented in this section to highlight their influential thought in African management.

P. Mufune—The Role of African Culture in Managerial Behavior

Mufune explored how values and approaches derived from African culture may or may not be affecting managers and the functioning of organizations. He examined how African managers diverge from managers in other countries. He concluded by emphasizing that many shortcomings remain in research on the African culture-managerial behavior dynamic (Mufune, 2003, pp. 17–28).

A. I. Ahiauzu—The African Thought System and the Work Behavior of the Industrial Man

Ahiauzu has studied and contrasted the work attitudes of African workers with their counterparts in industrialized settings. His studies have identified African indigenous thought system to be influenced by the use of symbols, common-sense knowledge, proverbs, and legends. Two major points concluded by Ahiauzu's studies are the facts that many of those holding supervisory and managerial positions have received their education and training based on Western thought, theories, and practices, and that most of the studies on the African industrial worker have been conducted by non-Africans. The problem this has presented is that they have both treated and viewed the African industrial worker based on the perception of Western values. He emphasized the importance of understanding the African worker from the perspective of African thought and values (Ahiauzu, 1986, pp. 37–58).

C. O. Nzelibe—The Evolution of African Management Thought

Nzelibe has posited that the underlying principles of management in Africa are quite different from those in the West. The core dimensions of modern African management thought include traditionalism, communalism, and cooperative teamwork. He has argued that the exclusion of such factors from African management practices and thinking has been responsible for managerial problems such as nepotism, bribery, corruption, and an acute lack of discipline in organizations, particularly in public servants (Nzelibe, 1986, pp. 6–16).

F. Abudu—Work Attitudes of Africans, With Special Reference to Nigeria

Abudu concluded in his research that many negative characteristics of the African workforce can be attributed to the absence of an industrial culture in Africa. He found that cultural expectations relative to work in traditional Africa did not emphasize commitment, diligence, and proper attitudes toward work. Consequently, the African became stereotyped as lazy, of low productivity, and unwilling to respond to economic incentives. In Africa, family is what defines a person. Abudu found that most Africans were unwilling to break away from the security of their family ties in search of employment in urban settings. These ties to family, coupled with the fear of illnesses and death in the urban areas, had influenced the European view of the "lazy African" (Abudu, 1986, pp. 17–36).

S. M. Nyambegera—Ethnicity and Human Resource Management Practice in Sub-Saharan Africa

Nyambegera explored issues of human resource diversity in the multiethnic societies of sub-Saharan Africa, arguing that ethnicity constitutes a primary dimension of diversity. He examined the influence of ethnicity on employment relations in organizational life in this region and explored whether the discourse of managing diversity could be applied effectively. He argued that if the ethnic diversity found in African organizations is well managed, it could enhance organizational harmony and effectiveness. Furthermore, if organizations in Africa deliberately embrace approaches of "inclusion" rather than "exclusion" in managing their human resources and appreciate the inherent employee "difference," the image and effectiveness of organizations operating here could improve. At the same time, he admitted the need to adapt such approaches to the cultural specificity of local contexts (Nyambegera, 2002, pp. 1077–1090).

Harvey Sindima—Liberalism and African Culture

Sindima wrote about the clash between Western and African culture. In particular, he contrasted individualism, which is prevalent in Western culture, with collectivism, which is prevalent in many African societies. He defined liberalism within the context of welfare state, or wealth and power. He viewed all three—wealth, power, and state—as manifestations of a mindset that centers on individualism. He posited that in liberalism, it is the individual, considered as an entity, who matters. This is counter to collectivist societies, which define the individual through the collective (Sindima, 1990, pp. 190–209).

M. L. Jones—Management Development With an African Focus and Managerial Thinking With an African Perspective

Jones has published empirical research concerning managerial thinking and development in Africa. His country of focus on the research referenced here has been Malawi. In particular, he has examined the complexity and controversy of importing management concepts developed in the West into African organizations. He has also concluded that managerial thinking and behavior can be influenced by powerful political systems and factors (Jones, 1988, pp. 481–505; Jones, 1989, pp. 74–90).

E. D. Prinsloo—The African View of Participatory Business Management

Prinsloo delineated the group of activities concerned with business and then discussed the concepts used by Ubuntu as an example of the African view of business management, identifying those activities regarded by Africans as being basic to their worldview. He showed how these Ubuntu concepts are applicable to business management, using the ideas of Lovemore Mbigi, who is an important advocate of the Ubuntu style of participatory management. Mbigi's Ubuntu-influenced views are centered on collectivism, participation, and sharing. In doing so, Prinsloo tried to establish what some important African thinkers themselves regard as the special position of Ubuntu in contrast to individualism, collectivism, and Western humanism (Prinsloo, 2000, pp. 275–286).

M. P. Mangaliso—Building Competitive Advantage from Ubuntu

Mangaliso examined the competitive advantages of Ubuntu by exploring the assumptions of relationships, language and communication, decision making, time, productivity, age and leadership, and belief systems (Mangaliso, 2001, pp. 23–33).

M. Masango—Leadership in the African Context

Masango explores the meaning of leadership by focusing on periods in African history that have made a lasting impact on Africans' conception of themselves and their society. He discusses the influence of Christianity and Islam on the people of Africa and the contention that the present social, economic, and political instability in Africa is the legacy of colonialism (Masango, 2003, pp. 313–321).

F. E. Obiakor—Building Patriotic African Leadership Through African-Centered Education

Obiakor sees Africa as a continent in transition. Its education, economy, politics, and society do not reflect 21st century trends. He sees African leadership as still tied to European-centered frameworks that are counterproductive to the sacred existence of African peoples. Rarely does good news come from Africa; problematic situations in self-governance are frequent. He proposes proactive, African-centered educational programs that could produce nationalistic and patriotic leadership willing to tackle Africa's endemic problems (Obiakor, 2004, pp. 402–420).

Rick James

James has written extensively about his experiences with OD in Africa. He has argued that the many principles of OD preexist in African cultures and are not a new, foreign import. He has concluded that "as with any culture, certain aspects undermine or reinforce particular approaches to management and change. An anthropological perspective can assist in understanding the local culture sufficiently to be able to identify, avoid, or overcome cultural resistance, while at the same time using cultural symbols as levers for change" (James, 2004, p. 313).

Chiku Malunga

Malunga has published a book on how to make strategic plans work based on African insights. He has also researched how to use African proverbs and metaphors to help organizations understand the theory and practice of strategic planning. Malunga has also published a book on understanding organizational leadership through Ubuntu. He has posited that Ubuntu offers a creative, innovative, and holistic approach to understanding organizational leadership by using the principles of Ubuntu (Malunga, 2009a, 2009b).

Lovemore Mbigi

Mbigi has researched and published on how to effectively utilize Ubuntu in human resource management and transformational management. He is one of the leading authorities on Ubuntu and is frequently cited in publications on Ubuntu. He has also researched African spirituality and storytelling, and shown how they are applicable in dealing with management issues.

Organization Development Practitioners

This section describes the work of some of the notable organization development practitioners in Africa. Many practitioners and consultants of organization development in Africa receive limited or no attention in the West. Their work is present here because of their views of organizational management and OD from the perspective of the African setting. Their biographical information is presented in this section to highlight their influential thought in African OD practice.

Chiku Malunga is a consultant and author with many years' experience in organization development work among African and European NGOs. He is currently the director of Capacity Development Consultants (CADECO), an organization that promotes African-centered organizational improvement models. His work includes understanding organizational sustainability through and organizational wisdom in African proverbs. He holds a doctorate in development studies from the University of South Africa.

Louw Du Toit has been a registered management and development consultant since 1979. He graduated with degrees in both mathematical and behavior sciences at the Rand Afrikaans University (now University of Johannesburg) and focused his postgraduate studies on business strategy and change management. After a career of nearly 10 years in the mining industry and later at Gencor, Louw left the corporate world to become a professional consultant. He started the firm Louw Du Toit and Associates in 1980. Apart from his work in the Republic of South Africa, he consults on projects and trains leaders in change management within the global context (e.g., United States, Canada, UK, Spain, Austria, Poland, Russia, Israel, and several countries in Africa). He has won the International Outstanding Consultant of the Year Award twice and has served on the advisory board of the Organization Development Institute (USA) since 1981. In South Africa, he participated in virtually all major transformational events until 2004. He has been focusing since then on positive survival strategies and capacity building for the future.

Warren Banks has worked for the past decade in the field of OD and change, mainly with development sector organizations. His main professional practice is process facilitation. He is particularly interested in supporting organizations to move through and past "stuckness" and to redefine their ways of being and working (strategy, structure, processes, and relationships). He also has a strong interest in personal and professional development processes.

Tsitsi Maradze is a development practitioner with 13 years of experience working especially with civil society organizations in southern and eastern Africa. Since 1999, she has provided services in organization development, change management, institutional development, project cycle management, strategic planning and management, leadership development, and capacity strengthening across diverse sectors in which civil society organizations work. Since 2007, she has also been a consultant to the World Bank, providing technical support and guidance to World Bank clients, including the Malawian and Zimbabwean governments, and facilitating capacity strengthening of World Bank staff in some of the countries in Africa.

Loretta van Schalkwyk is a seasoned personal and organizational development practitioner and mediator. Over a career span of 40 years, Loretta has acquired extensive experience in the fields of leadership, management, organizational development and change, training, facilitation, mentoring, and values-based life coaching. Her work has involved interaction with corporate, government, and trade union groupings and, in more recent years, the nonprofit sector.

Hestern Banda is a well-respected professional consultant in organizational development, management, and social development. A professional consultant, he has experience in conducting strategic plans, strategic reviews, and evaluations of programs and projects in various fields, including human rights and good governance. He is a member of the International Organizational Development Association and serves on several international boards of directors, including an NGO called Partners in Hope, which provides choice HIV/AIDS and medical care and services in Malawi. He is also a certified World Bank Community-Driven Development Distance-Learning Facilitator and Trainer of Trainers.

Davine Thaw was a farm manager, became a sociologist, and set up the successful NGO Olive-Organization Development and Training, which specializes in organizational development work in the NGO sector. She is a facilitator and an entrepreneur, dedicated to development and related policies. She recently became a freelance consultant and works in Europe and Africa.

Rick James has worked in NGO management for more than 20 years, primarily in Latin America, Africa, and Europe. After working for a Honduran NGO for 4 years, he completed an MBA in the UK and has been with INTRAC since 1992. James has trained, consulted, researched, and written extensively on NGO capacity building and organizational change issues. He spent 10 years with INTRAC in Malawi, where he trained a team of Malawian OD practitioners, provided capacity-building support to Malawian NGO support organizations, undertook research into leadership change issues, and consulted for international NGOs on the monitoring and evaluation of capacity building. He has a PhD in NGO management, focusing on OD and leadership development with NGOs in Africa.

Joyce Mataya, primarily an organizational development practitioner, has been with CABUNGO, a capacity-building organization based in Malawi, since its inception in 1997. Joyce has been in the NGO sector since 1995 and has worked with a number of nongovernmental organizations.

Leonard Satali is an experienced community development facilitator and environmentalist. He has experience in training organizations and project teams in project planning and implementation, facilitation of organizational assessment processes, strategic planning and thinking, systems and procedures review and development, structure review and development, and roles and responsibilities clarification.

Consulting Organizations

A number of NGOs and private consulting organizations provide OD services in the southern region of Africa. Highlighted here is the work of such organizations making an impact in organizations and communities in southern Africa with change management strategies, capacity building, training, research, and OD.

The Christian Organizations Research and Advisory Trust for Africa (CORAT Africa) is a pan-African, not-for-profit, Christian organization established in March 1975. The original purpose of CORAT was enabling effective leadership, management, and accountability of churches and church-related organizations in a Christian and professional manner. The institution has continued to offer consultancy services in the areas of long-term organization development processes, organizational assessments and development, strategic planning and management, capacity building, program and project evaluations, feasibility studies, needs assessments, and research and publications (www.coratafrica.com).

EASUN facilitates organization development for civil society organizations, helping them become aware of their values and vision as the basis for their ethical growth and effectiveness. To this end, EASUN offers leadership training, change management support, and other activities for institutional development of civil society organizations in East Africa (www.easun-tz.org).

Community Development Resource Association of South Africa is a South African NGO that is a center for organizational innovation and developmental practice. The organization does research, training, and OD consultancy (www.cdra.org.za).

CABUNGO, also known as Capacity Building Organization, is a Malawian organization that provides OD services to organizations doing development work. It is a consultancy service provider whose major services include developing strategic plans, governance, proposal development, team building, time management, systems and policy development, and leadership-development training. It has 10 years of providing OD services (www.cabungo.org).

CADECO is a Malawian-based organizational consultancy firm that helps organizations to improve their performance through the provision of OD interventions. It facilitates OD interventions and OD training programs and develops effective networks and OD publications (www.cadeco.mw).

INTRAC is a not-for-profit organization based in Oxford, working to strengthen civil society and development aid policy and practice through training, research, and capacity- building interventions (www.intrac.org).

Empirical Studies of OD in Southern Africa

What has been encouraging is the broad level of empirical research that is being conducted in the field of management and OD in southern Africa. A review of the literature in Malawi and South Africa from the late 1980s to

2010 demonstrates the growing importance of OD approaches in resolving organizational issues. The reference to culture in these studies has been critical in viewing organizational issues not only from an African perspective but also from a subcultural context. A table with these empirical studies is provided in the appendix section for the reader.

Summary

The chapter began with the literature review on the evolutionary background and development of OD as a field. Because *organization development* is sometimes used in contexts in which it is limited, a literature review of OD helped to clarify its definition and application. The evolutionary path of its development was influenced by key scholars of behavioral sciences, psychologists, as well as practitioners. The chapter also addressed the stems of OD as part of its evolutionary development. The second half of the chapter discussed the introduction of the field in southern Africa. The introduction of the field in this part of the African continent has been led by international nongovernmental organizations and civil society organizations. The chapter recognized some of the African scholars who have researched and published on management topics from an African perspective. Some of the local African OD practitioners are also recognized primarily as potential partners for those with an interest in working in southern Africa. The chapter concluded with a brief discussion of the literature review of empirical studies of OD and management in Malawi and South Africa. The literature review is referenced in this chapter to demonstrate the growing interest in using OD to resolve organization issues. This book views culture as an important component for applying OD techniques in southern Africa. The next chapter explores values and assumptions of culture in southern Africa.

References

Abudu, F. (1986). Work attitudes of Africans, with special reference to Nigeria. *International Studies of Management & Organization, 16*(2), 17–36.

Ahiauzu, A. I. (1986). The African thought-system and the work behavior of the African industrial man. *International Studies of Management & Organization, 16*(2), 37–58.

Alderfer, C. (1977). Organization development. *Annual Review of Psychology, 28*(1), 197–223.

Burke, W. W. (2006). Where did OD come from? In J. V. Gallos (Ed.), *Organization development.* San Francisco, CA: Jossey-Bass.

Cummings, T. G., & Worley, C. G. (2005). *Organization development and change* (8th ed.). Mason, OH: Thomson South-Western.

French, W. L., & Bell, C. H. (1999). *Organization development: Behavioral science intervention for organization improvement.* Englewood Cliffs, NJ: Prentice Hall.

Gallos, J. V. (Ed.). (2006). *Organization development: A Jossey-Bass reader.* San Francisco, CA: Jossey-Bass.

Hatch, M. J., & Cunliffe, A. L. (2004). *Organization theory: Modern, symbolic, and postmodern perspectives* (2nd ed.). New York, NY: Oxford University Press.

James, R. (2004). Exploring OD in Africa: A response to David Lewis. *Nonprofit Management & Leadership, 14*(3), 313–324.

Jones, M. (1988). Managerial thinking: An African perspective. *Journal of Management Studies, 25*(5), 481–505.

Jones, M. L. (1989). Management development: An African focus. *International Studies of Management & Organization, 19*(1), 74–90.

Malunga, C. (2009a). *Making strategic plans work: Insights from African indigenous wisdom.* London: Adonis & Abbey.

Malunga, C. (2009b). *Understanding organizational leadership through Ubuntu.* London: Adonis & Abbey.

Mangaliso, M. P. (2001). Building competitive advantage from Ubuntu: Management lessons from South Africa. *Academy of Management Executive, 15*(3), 23–33.

Masango, M. (2003). Leadership in the African context. *Ecumenical Review, 55*(4), 313–321.

Mirvis, P. H. (1988). Organization development: Part I—An evolutionary perspective. *Research in Organization Change and Development, 2,* 1–57.

Mirvis, P. H. (1990). Organization development: Part II—A revolutionary perspective. *Research in Organization Change and Development, 4,* 1–66.

Mufune, P. (2003). African culture and managerial behavior: Clarifying the connections. *South African Journal of Business Management, 34*(3), 17–28.

Ndegwa, S. N. (2001). A decade of democracy in Africa. *Journal of Asian & African Studies (Brill), 36*(1), 1–16.

Nyambegera, S. M. (2002). Ethnicity and human resource management practice in sub-Saharan Africa: The relevance of the managing diversity discourse. *International Journal of Human Resource Management, 13*(7), 1077–1090.

Nzelibe, C. O. (1986). The evolution of African management thought. *International Studies of Management & Organization, 16*(2), 6–16.

Obiakor, F. E. (2004). Building patriotic African leadership through African-centered education. *Journal of Black Studies, 34*(3), 402–420.

Prinsloo, E. D. (2000). The African view of participatory business management. *Journal of Business Ethics, 25*(4), 275–86.

Roubini, N. (1997). Supply side economics. *Stern School of Business, New York University.* Retrieved from http://pages.stern.nyu.edu/~nroubini/SUPPLY.HTM#act1

Sankara, T. (1985). Retrieved from http://en.wikiquote.org/wiki/Thomas_Sankara

Sindima, H. (1990). Liberalism and African culture. *Journal of Black Studies, 21*(2), 190–209.

Stavros, J. (1998) *Capacity building: An appreciative approach.* Published dissertation. Case Western Reserve University, Cleveland, OH.

Taylor, F. W. (1915). *The principles of scientific management.* New York, NY: Harper & Row.

Watson, R., & Collingwood, C. (2008). *Final evaluation of Intrac Malawi Programme 1998–2007: Strengthening civil society in Malawi.* CORDAID, unpublished.

Weisbord, M. R. (2004). *Productive workplaces revisited: Dignity, meaning, and community in the 21st century.* San Francisco, CA: Jossey-Bass.

2

Underlying Assumptions and Values of Southern African Culture

You can never change society if you have not changed yourself.
—Nelson Mandela

Why is culture important? How do we effectively define culture in Africa when what has been written about it over the years has been done so in a negative light and from the perspective of the West? How do we discuss a rich and diverse culture that has historically been defined in monolithic terms as a result of colonialism and misrepresentation? How do we define African cultures within the context of globalization? And how does national culture influence organizational culture and behavior?

These are indeed important questions to consider when we begin to discuss culture within the African context. Culture is what defines who we are as a people, how we function within society, what beliefs and values we hold, which traditions we practice, what structures we recognize, how we communicate, what rites and ceremonies we perform, and how we raise our families. We choose to share our culture with others in different ways. This chapter discusses both modes of communication and structures that

Creating Opportunities for Change and OD in Southern Africa, pages 25–46

are embedded within culture to help define it from an African perspective. Culture in this chapter will be identified through leadership models, belief systems, political systems and experience, the use of metaphors and proverbs, storytelling, and cultural frameworks.

Diversity of African Culture

Africa's languages, customs, traditions, and rites are diverse. African culture is thus not monolithic. This point is critical because cultural models may not always take such diversities in societies into consideration. In Malawi for instance, Chewa customs are going to differ from Tumbuka customs. The Tumbukas practice *lobola* (paying a price to the bride's family), while the Chewa do not. The Chewa people have rites of passage that involve the *Gulewamkulu* (masked dancers), other ethnic groups do not. The Yao, who are predominantly Muslims, have *jando* (circumcision) as part of their rite of passage. These distinctions among the various ethnic groups also exist within their community structures, and although similarities may help to define the national culture, it is important to understand the differences as well. Those differences may prove to be useful, particularly when OD practitioners are working in a region that has a dominant ethnic group. Assuming a certain type of culture based on a single cultural model may prove to be counterproductive in facilitating organizational change.

Leadership Models

It is important to understand African leadership in the context of culture, management practices, and tolerance for change. What is African leadership? Is there such a term as African leadership given Africa's broad and diverse setting? What types of leadership models exist in Africa? How do African leadership models align with the values of OD? Masango (2003) defines African leadership through the groups they lead. If the group performs well, then the leader is deemed to be effective (p. 315). Masango claims that even with Africa's diversity, similarities in culture exist, particularly with respect to leadership.

The transitional history of the continent of Africa has had an impact on its development of leadership. The historical periods discussed in this chapter provide the background for the development and definition of leadership in Africa. This section describes three leadership models and then discusses the types of leadership that have developed in Africa as a result of its transitional history.

Traditional Leadership Model

Traditional leaders have had a presence in African societies during all transitional eras. African societies have been organized into clusters along tribal and ethnic lines for centuries. These clusters have been defined as kingdoms, clans, villages, and traditional authorities. At the helm of these clusters are rulers whose families have traditionally been in the position of dispensing authority. Their roles over the years have ranged from military leaders, as was the case with King Shaka of the Zulu kingdom and Emperor Haile Salaise of modern Ethiopia, to more ceremonial and cultural roles, as in the case of King Mswati of Swaziland and many chiefs in other parts of Africa. These cluster leaders have also played judicial roles for infractions that were more cultural, and they are the keepers of their cluster's traditions and beliefs. According to Masango (2003), "African people treat a leader by virtue of being a king, priest or ruler chosen by virtue of the office in order to serve the nation" (p. 313).

These cluster leaders, particularly in Malawi, are often surrounded by a council of advisers who assist in adjudication and the dispensation of authority. They hold titles such as king of kings (Inkosi ya ma Kosi), chief (Mfumu), queen (Ndlobvukazi), village headman (Nyakwawa), and adviser to the court (Induna). Malunga (2009) notes that "While a king in Africa was the most visible leader and the indigenous custodian of power, auxiliary authorities—often people of highly respected religious or elder status—continually advised the king in roles that promoted democracy in the kingdom" (p. 63). Malunga calls this structure value-based leadership. There have been attempts to erode or weaken these traditional roles during the transitional eras because they have been viewed as a threat or impediment to control by religious and political movements. However, these leadership structures are still thriving amidst an environment that has changed dramatically over the years.

Transformational Leadership Model

The transformational leadership model emerged during the third era (1960s), when colonized Africa was breaking away from the clutches of colonialism. Transformational leadership defines a type of leadership that creates voluble and positive change in its followers. The leader transforms and motivates followers by charisma, intellectual arousal, and individual consideration. In addition, this leader seeks new working ways, trying to identify new opportunities versus threats, to advance beyond the status quo, and to alter the environment (Dionne, Yammarino, Atwater, & Spangler,

2004; Garcia-Morales, Matías-Reche, & Hurtado-Torres, 2008; Judge & Piccolo, 2004; Pillai & Williams, 2004; Vecchio, Justin, & Pearce, 2008). This model of leadership has been at the center of most large systems' change, which has resulted in new dispensations of government or significant cultural shifts in Africa. For example, when Malawi and other African countries embarked on the journey for independence in the late 1950s and early 1960s, transformational figures were chosen to lead these independence movements and large-systems change efforts. In the case of Malawi, Dr. Kamuzu Banda, a Western-educated physician, returned to Malawi to lead his country to independence. Other notable transformational leaders of the independence movements were Nelson Mandela (South Africa), Kwame Nkrumah (Ghana), Julius Nyerere (Tanzania), Kenneth Kaunda (Zambia), Patrice Lumumba (Zaire/Congo), Jomo Kenyatta (Kenya), and Robert Mugabe (Zimbabwe). It is indeed highly notable that these figures were synonymously revered with new-found statehood.

Authoritarian Leadership Model

An interesting dynamic that occurred, particularly with the transformational figures of Africa (except for Nelson Mandela), was their transition into authoritarian figures. Most of these leaders reflect the paradoxical nature of Africa by being champions for democracy prior to independence and suppressors of democracy in the postindependence period. Jones (1989) states,

> Dr. Banda became President (and in 1971 was made the Life President) of the new Republic of Malawi. The story of Dr. Banda's apparently historic destiny in liberating the country of his birth from its colonial masters is extraordinary, and his continued dominance as a leader of Malawi is an overwhelming factor in the nation's development. (p. 71)

Subsequent to independence, Malawi and most of the countries south of the Sahara had systems of government that were authoritarian in nature over an extended period of time, which consequently had an impact on organizational management and behavior.

Influence of Political Systems on Culture

Political systems have an influence on the national and organizational culture. If a country is founded on democratic principles, to some extent, those principles become embedded into the culture of that particular country. This does not mean that all democratic countries have democratic organizations. What it does mean is that the political system has some influence on the culture. Much of the reinforcement of the political system is done through the laws governing that particular country. Over time, those laws become part of the culture, at least for that period of time.

Apartheid Culture

Take, for instance, the system of Apartheid, which was the political system in South Africa from 1948 to 1994. During that time, laws were passed that helped to reinforce that particular system of government. Over time, Apartheid became acculturated in South Africa even though it was politically and socially rejected by Blacks and a few White South Africans. Organizationally, South African-based organizations reflected the system and structure of Apartheid. As long as there were laws to reinforce Apartheid, the culture of the country was influenced by the political system. It takes a long time to change culture, particularly national culture, because it so embedded in the psyche of the people. Even 17 years after Apartheid's end, remnants remain in South Africa today: poor Black South Africans still feel marginalized and separated from the main economic system. Socially, some Blacks have successfully climbed the corporate ladder, but more needs to be done. New laws have been passed to reverse Apartheid practices, but it will take time to change the culture of Apartheid.

Authoritarianism in Malawi

Malawi's political system started as a democracy after the country gained independence in 1964. Like most of the countries in Southern Africa, it did not take long for the government that had led the country to independence to become autocratic. Led by the late Dr. Hastings Kamuzu Banda, Malawi officially became a one-party state in 1966, when a new constitution was adopted. Dr. Banda consolidated his power when he was declared President for Life in 1971. For the next 23 years, the party and government of Dr. Banda successfully embedded its political structure into the culture of the Malawian people. It did so by deliberately portraying itself through Malawian symbols, rituals, values, and basic assumptions.

The government ensured that images of Dr. Banda appeared in every aspect of Malawian livelihood. His imposing portrait stared out in businesses, public buildings, and the homes of ordinary Malawians. The absence of his portrait in one's home was viewed as unpatriotic and almost treasonous. Whenever the president held public meetings, the people came out wearing cloth emblazoned with his image. Traditional songs reserved for ceremonies and rites of passage were changed to sing the praises of Kamuzu, the "hero." Certain situations were assumed and understood by the people as being contrary to the position of the government. For instance, Malawians could not discuss the president's age because culturally it is not polite to discuss the age of the elderly. Discussing his age was thus forbidden by law. Malawians could not entertain the thought of having another leader besides Kamuzu. These assumptions were also expectations. Malawians who were born under this system of government had no other frame of reference. Even though there were laws to reinforce the government's position on the people, many Malawians, particularly from the pre-Kamuzu era, paid the ultimate price for freedom when the time came to get rid of his autocratic regime.

The government's influence on the national culture trickled down to organizational culture. Many of the corporations were led by individuals who were directly affiliated with the government. They brought to those corporations the political culture that was propagated by the government. The culture of fear and the lack of tolerance for diverse views that existed politically were also prevalent organizationally. Thus, anyone attempting to facilitate change within the organization needed to appreciate the Malawian culture, not just in the anthropological sense but also in how the culture was influenced politically.

The political culture led by Kamuzu's government manifested itself in the national culture. It took 30 years for that culture to become the Malawian culture. Even though Kamuzu's government was ousted in 1994 to give way to a pluralistic form of government, that culture still has a presence in Malawian society today. Although there have been two other administrations since Kamuzu, some of the oppressive views from the Kamuzu era remain. This supports the argument that it takes a long time to change culture. James (2004), said, "In Malawi, for example, the cultural expectations of how decisions are made are still dominated by the legacy of President Kamuzu Banda's thirty-year dictatorship, in which fear and punishment were the main tools for leadership" (p. 319).

Malawi today is going through political turmoil because the government is attempting to limit civil liberties through the adoption of oppressive laws. Civil societies have taken the position that there seems to be a reversion to the political culture of the Kamuzu era. Did the culture ever change with the ousting of Kamuzu in 1994? Do the oppressed mimic the oppressor? How long before the autocratic culture gets replaced with a more democratic culture? How can one engage an organization in organizational change when the culture is autocratic? These are critical questions for further thought and research on the subject of political culture. It is important for OD practitioners to understand the political history of a given country in Africa because of its influence on the culture. Understanding the political culture may be a survival issue for OD practitioners in some countries.

African Belief Systems and Culture

Spirituality and belief systems are part of African culture and societies. Not only is spirituality in Africa defined through organized religious institutions such as Christianity and Islam, but it is prevalent in rites and ceremonies that have been in place for many years. The belief in ancestral spirits, the supernatural, superstition, and animism still influences most Africans today. According to Mbigi (2000), "In African spirit religion, the spirit represents our ultimate real self, our inner self and total being, and our total consciousness. The spirit is who we really are" (p. 36).

The presence of this belief system in African societies was seen as a threat by Christian missionaries, who discouraged its recognition and practice as being paganism. Concerted attempts were made to erode these practices, rites, and ceremonies through Western cultural indoctrination. What the missionaries failed to understand was that these belief systems were deeply embedded in the culture of African societies.

Why are belief systems important from an OD perspective? The answer is twofold. First, some Western cultural practices may be considered to be taboo in a particular African society. It is important to know what those are so as not to offend anyone. Second, opportunities may exist for leveraging spirituality with OD. For instance, Mbigi (2000) has developed a model that uses the African spirit hierarchy to manage an organization's emotional and spiritual resources.

Using Metaphors and Proverbs in Communicating Cultural Values

Proverbs, metaphors, and storytelling are an important means to understanding culture in Africa. According to James (2004), these sayings and customs predicate that OD values have had a presence in Africa long before OD was exported there and indigenized:

> Anthropologists have highlighted that one important way to gain insight into a culture is through its stories and proverbs. It is clear from the proverbs that are used in Malawi that many of the "new OD ideas from the West" are not new or Western at all, but have been around for centuries. The need for

> teamwork and participative decision making was recognized in Malawian culture well before OD appeared on the scene. (p. 321)

A review of the literature on management and OD in Africa presented some of these African metaphors as descriptors of societies with collective attributes.

Ubuntu ungamuntu mgabunye abantu—You do not live for yourself; you live for others (Ali et al., 2001, p. 59).
Kugona pakati nkuyambira—To sleep in the middle (of the group, where it is warmest) is to be first (Ali et al., 2001, p. 60).
Akufuna akhale ndani—What does she/he want to be (Ali et al., 2001, p. 61)?
Akudziyesa kuti ndi ndani—Who does she/he think she/he is (Ali et al., 2001, p. 61)?
Mutu umodzi siusenza denga—One pillar cannot support the roof structure on its own (Ali et al., 2001, p. 60).
Collective fingers theory—A thumb working on its own is useless (Swartz & Davies, 1997, p. 291).

These metaphors and proverbs are rejections of the individualistic attributes within society. They support the argument that African culture, particularly in Malawi and South Africa, is more collectivist than individualistic. If individuals try to excel outside the context of the group or the community, they are pulled back by society. This concept is defined by Ali et al. (2001) as the "pull down motive." These metaphorical arguments, even though societal, further define the collectivist approach to management within organizations. In a study of Malawian managers intended to highlight the correlation between national cultures and organizational behavior, Jones (1989) observed "an emphasis on prestige and status differences, creating relationships of dependency, which in organizations finds expression in wide differentials between organizational levels, particularly between managers and workers" (p. 81). He further noted that in a collectivist society such as the one that exists in Malawi, managers view their subordinates as

> a network of people rather than as human resources; in an emphasis on maintaining relationships rather than on providing opportunities for individual development... and in a reluctance by managers either to accept individual blame for mistakes or to criticize individual subordinates in a direct manner. (p. 81)

In Malawi, collectivism is reinforced by beliefs in witchcraft. Individual accomplishments or calamities in a work setting are attributable to witchcraft. According to Ali et al. (2001), "Malawians often view success and failure as caused by traditional spirits (Chizimba); and thus may seek traditional protective spells before accepting a promotion, or even turn down the promotion altogether for fear of its social consequences" (p. 62).

African societies are culturally loyal to their leadership, which in turn creates a paradox with the notion of equity because loyalty to their leaders may foster inequity between leader and followers. The dimension of power distance is fostered through the use of proverbs, such as the following from the Chewa tribe of Malawi, cited by James (2002b):

Atambala awiri salira mkhola limodzi—Two cocks do not crow in one kraal. (There can only be one leader, so if others are talking they are competing with the leader.)

Mutu ukakula sulewa mkhonya—A big head will not dodge the fists. (The leader is responsible for sorting out all our problems.)

Chalaka bakha nkhuku singatole—If a duck with a long beak cannot pick it up, then a chicken certainly cannot. (If a leader cannot solve something, then the followers certainly cannot.)

Wamkulu sawuzidwa—He is old . . . therefore he is right. (A leader's decision is not open for discussion.)

Using African Proverbs and Storytelling in Organization Development

Besides being descriptors of culture, proverbs are used in African societies when dispensing judgment in an indigenous court setting. The court system in countries like Malawi consists of two parallel systems. The first system is based on what was inherited from the British colonialists. The second system is more indigenously developed through traditional African courts. It is within this setting that a chief who may function as a judge may use proverbs to support his decision and dispense judgment. Proverbs may also be used for teaching good behavior, respect, empathy, resiliency, and survival. On the other hand, proverbs can also be used to warn others of calamity befalling them if their behavior is not consistent with cultural values. Finally, proverbs are used to provide advice on appropriate cultural values and mores within a society.

A story is typically associated with a particular proverb, helping to provide context and meaning to the proverb. This association is similar to Jesus

Christ's parables in the Bible, which were lessons he taught with storytelling. This section contains examples of Malawian proverbs with supporting stories. The proverbs will then be further described within an OD context.

Chikomekome Cha Nkhuyu M'kati Muli Nyerere

A delicious looking fruit may be infested with ants inside. There was a person who had embarked on a long journey. After traveling for some time, he started to feel the pangs of hunger. Unfortunately, he had not brought any food with him on this long journey. Suddenly he came across a giant fruit tree that had ripened and delicious looking fruit strewn around it. He was so happy of this discovery because he realized that his hunger was to be no more. He picked the biggest and most ripened fruit from the ground. When he took a bite of the giant fruit, he discovered that it was infested with ants. He tried to pick others from the ground, but the result was the same. He was saddened because he realized that he had been fooled by the look of the fruit, not knowing that inside the fruit was an infestation of ants.

This particular proverb has similar meaning to two Western proverbs: "All that glitters is not gold" and "Do not judge a book by its cover." This proverb can be used to advise organizations planning to hire OD consultants to be cautious of consultants who might spend too much time tooting their own horns. These could be consultants with flashy websites, fancy titles, and catchy names. In some cases, these consultants may lack the substance the organization needs to change and develop. The same proverb could also be used to further the theme of this book, that not all ideas and concepts generated in the West are good for Africa. Many ideas and concepts are readily embraced by African organizations because they have the Western allure. The problem here is that some of these Western ideas may clash with African cultural values if indigenization is not applied.

Nguluwe Idalira Msampha Utaning'a

The boar cried out when it was ensnared in the trap. A hunter went out in the bush to set up his trap. The next day his trap ensnared a wild boar. The wild boar tried to free itself from the trap all day long since the hunter had not checked on his trap. The wild boar's efforts started to loosen the trap. However, when it got dark, the wild boar became afraid and started to cry out aloud. These cries alerted the hunter that his trap had ensnared an animal. He rushed over to the spot where he had set up the trap and killed the wild boar. The wild boar was thus killed by the hunter just before it managed to set itself free from the trap.

The lesson with this proverb is that it is better to persevere during difficult times than to give up. One may give too up too soon when triumph or relief is around the corner. The process of change in any context and setting is very difficult and hard. Change can be chaotic and bring about anxiety and fear. This proverb emphasizes the importance of perseverance when times are tough. To develop resiliency, one has to persevere through very difficult times.

Myang'ana Dzuwa Adasokera

The sun gazer got lost. There was a young man who wanted to find a job in a town where the sun set. He had not visited this place before. However, since this place was located where the sun set, he thought that it would be easy to find. He planned on following the sun to reach his destination. He bid farewell to his parents and relatives. They advised him to ask for directions so that he would not get lost. He embarked on his journey at dawn heading north. When the sun came out, he had travelled for several miles. He had a difficult journey because when lost, he refused to ask for directions. He was too proud to ask for directions because he thought any smart person should know the place where the sun sets. After traveling for several days, he lost hope that he would reach his destination. After several days of wandering through many villages, he decided to return home. It was not going to be that easy for him to retrace his footsteps back home because he passed through many villages. He convinced himself to retrace his steps by following the direction where the sun rose. After traveling for several days he was completely lost.

The lesson of this proverb is that for those who don't ask for guidance or advice for fear of getting embarrassed may find themselves in precarious situations. Organizations develop their own cultures as a subtext of national culture. Global consultants cannot assume that they know the culture of a country because they have read and studied it. Reading and studying it is not the same as living it. If one is to successfully work in another culture, seeking help from a local person greatly contributes to that success. In some cases, utilizing that local guidance could save your life or reputation. On the other hand, there are many organizations that fail because they are too proud to ask for assistance.

Tsoka Sasimba Koma Mwayi

We cannot always talk of triumphing over danger, but we can always count our blessings. A long time ago, the hare and antelope were very close friends. They spent a lot of time together and shared everything. One day, when the two were hanging out, the antelope commented to the hare that he had heard of danger. He had never seen nor experienced any danger. He was curious to feel what it was like to be in danger. The hare cautioned his friend about playing or flirting with danger because it could result in death. The hare was talking from past experience when he had survived being trapped by hunters. He went on to state that he has lived to talk about it because he was blessed. The antelope wanted to have the same experience, the experience of triumphing over danger. The hare warned his friend about danger to no avail. The hare went into the bush to tell the lion that he was planning on delivering a great meal to him that evening. The lion was grateful but warned the hare that if he did not deliver this meal to him, he was going to eat the hare instead. The hare went back to the antelope to explain that he had met with danger in the bush. The antelope was flabbergasted that the hare lived to tell about it. He was more doubtful of the riskiness involved with danger. The hare told the antelope to accompany him to the bush that evening so that he could meet danger for the first time. When it was time, the hare and the antelope went into the bush. As they got closer to the place where the lion was hiding, the hare stood back. The antelope went further, still doubtful that he was going to meet with danger. When the lion saw that the antelope had moved close enough, he pounced and grabbed him. As the antelope was caught in the jaws of the lion, he cried out to the hare for help. The hare told him that what he was experiencing was the danger he had told him about. The lion subsequently ate the antelope.

The lesson behind this proverb is that we should not persist in doing things we know could be detrimental to us. Sometimes, for organizations to change and develop, they may have to take risks. They may know and understand the consequences of their risk and make their decisions to move forward based on that. Risks could be detrimental to an organization. As long as an organization understands what it is getting into in terms of risk, it may work out in the end. However, if the risks outweigh the benefits, then the organization could be in jeopardy of its existence.

Indigenization

Organization development, like other Western-developed concepts and theories, has over the years been defined in the context of Africa's multiple dimensions of culture, economics, and politics. Thus, much emphasis has been placed on the indigenization and hybridization of OD and management practices in order for their applicability to be sustainable in Africa. Edoho (2001) argued,

> African management philosophy should be concerned about the managerial ideas, thinking, and practices that are firmly rooted in the material experience, belief systems, normative values, culture and generally ways of life of the African people in their own settings. African based management philosophy must focus on the application of indigenous knowledge systems to facilitate the achievement of the triple objectives of economic, political and social development. This does not foreclose the opportunity often attributed to borrowed ideas, but that such ideas must have resonance with the framework of African thinking. (p. 74)

Indigenization, or hybridization, is therefore the localization of management practices based on culture for their sustainability. In other words, the importation of management practices, change processes, or administration from the West has to be infused or converged with local African culture for them to be sustainable. Proponents of African management systems have argued that the importation of Western management practices that are grounded in individualistic approaches have come into conflict with local African culture that is grounded in collectivist approaches and values. According to Thomas and Bendixen (2000),

> Management practice in South Africa is strongly modeled on British and American systems. Critics of such practice view the values underlying management practice and, indeed, organizational culture itself, as being northern European/British and at odds with values held by African managers who increasingly occupy positions in the business hierarchy. (p. 509)

Can we still call it OD if it adapts to local conditions? Is adaptability a compromise of OD values? Golembiewski (1991) argues,

> Neither OD designs nor cultures are homogenous; and change objectives differ radically from case to case in their urgency and acceptable probabilities of success, with each case requiring judgments to be made about closeness of fit. The available literature tends to oversimplify in posing such questions as:
>
> - Is OD exclusively culturally appropriate to North America?
> - Does nation A have a culture that constitutes a close fit to OD values/interventions?
> - Are close fits preferable to distal fits? (p. 40)

Golembiewski's studies have proven that even in the most inhospitable conditions for OD based on incongruence of culture and economics, some level of success has been achieved. This success supports his argument that OD practitioners do make reasonable adjustments or adaptation to local conditions in order for OD to be successful. Cultural sensitivity and awareness need to be taken into consideration when doing global OD. The models developed by Hofstede (1980), Hofstede and Hofstede (2005), and Jaeger (1984a, 1984b, 1986) help us understand cultural contexts. Golembiewski (1991) has argued that a closeness of fit is not a guarantee of success.

Other Western management thinkers such as Blunt (1995) and Jones and Mann (1983) have argued that establishing closeness of fit with OD in Africa is difficult because of Africa's cultural dimensions' being incongruent with OD values. James (2004) has summarized their argument:

> Not only is OD a foreign approach to managing change in Africa, but it also is not cross-culturally transferable... because OD processes evolved largely from experience with commercial firms in the United States.... OD values and assumptions about openness, collaboration, and expression of feelings do not fit many non-western cultures. (p. 316)

According to James (2004), these researchers feel that developing countries are less amenable to OD because they are characterized by high power distance and high uncertainty avoidance (p. 316). These Western thinkers state that African culture is inhospitable to OD because the culture itself discourages innovation, individualism, and openness—elements that are associated with the values of OD.

However, others have suggested that the argument for closeness of fit has resided mainly in the academic arena and that there needs to be a balance with the practitioner's experience in Africa (James, 2004, p. 318). James listed reasons practitioners have found relevance for OD in Africa:

> 1. While there are undoubted hindrances to OD in some African cultures, often these constraints are more about the way in which OD is implemented and the language used rather than the approach itself. Cultural and anthropological insights assist in avoiding potential pitfalls.
> 2. There are preexisting elements in many African cultures that promote rather than resist an OD approach to change. It can be argued that OD existed in Africa before it was imported and called OD. As a result, many cultural symbols and practices can be used as important levers for change. (pp. 318–319)

In support of these arguments, Murrell (1986) suggested that OD provides a relevant approach to bringing Africa out of its current environment of perpetual pessimism. He argued,

> OD, as it represents a set of values that stress the importance of participative change directed and led from within the system, is a natural for a developing country context. Local government sovereignty is to be respected as well as the rights and responsibilities of local citizens to manage the changes occurring in their societies. OD is by design the approach which in its flexible and organic nature allows for adaptation to local cultural conditions. (p. 53)

James (2004) posited that non-African writers are responsible for much of the arguments against OD. He felt that such writers failed to appreciate the many differences between and even within African cultures. He also argued that many "fail to distinguish between poor implementation of OD and the nature of OD per se" (p. 317).

James (2004) claimed that, in fact, OD's values align with African culture rather than diverge from it. Indigenously developed approaches to change have been practiced in Africa long before Western-developed OD approaches were imported on the continent (p. 320).

It is important to distinguish indigenization of OD from global OD. Global OD is the ability to apply this process for organizational change and development in other parts of the world while taking into account the cultural, political, economic, and social characteristics. The key to the success of global OD is based on how well OD change agents understand these national characteristics or values and are able to effectively prescribe interventions that are implementable and appropriate. Najafbagy (1990) raised the following issue:

> [P]rojects and technical assistance provided to Third World Countries do not take cultural and social factors into consideration. Many project incompatibilities have arisen from inadequate attention to and lack of or fit with, existing socio-cultural conditions. Development programmes without social and cultural considerations have either failed, or have had very little impact on the quality of life. (p. 62)

Since OD was founded in the United States with European influences, one could argue that its values are very much Western influenced and that these values may not necessarily be accepted in other parts of the world. The challenge for global OD practitioners then has been facilitating change in settings that have characteristics different from their own backgrounds while upholding the stated OD values. To help global OD practitioners or change agents facilitate change and development, Chapter 4, Cultural Models, discusses three cultural models developed by Hofstede, Binet, and the Ubuntu philosophy and provides context on how OD continues to be affected by cultural dimensions and constructs and, more importantly, how knowledge of these influences can allow for effective global OD to occur.

As defined for global OD, indigenization is the convergence of OD with local cultural attributes. This convergence has to occur with the input of local change agents or by the local change agents themselves. Golembiewski (1991) supported indigenization by arguing that culture and OD are not homogeneous and therefore that OD's adaptability is critical for success. The challenge for indigenization is that the literature presents little data to support correlation with success rates. Much has been covered in the literature on the need to localize OD or management practices for sustainability. However, according to Ali et al. (2001), imported and indigenous theories have yet to be fully tested in Africa and their sustainability measured (p. 60). Jones (1989) has asked a provocative question:

> Will the importation of management concepts and practices from the industrialized West meet Africa's needs? Questions concerning the transferability across nations of management concepts and practices are complex and controversial. There is as yet no consensus about the nature of arguments involved or about how empirical data can usefully be obtained and compared. (p. 75)

Indigenization is used because of the immediate recognition of local culture and other settings. Indigenization is preferred to global OD because of its empowerment of local managers and OD practitioners to converge Western-developed concepts with local cultures. Moreover, indigenization recognizes indigenously developed concepts as key management approaches.

The African Renaissance

Africa has had to contend with an element of pessimism brought about by overwhelming problems. OD has been presented as a means to assist African countries within different settings and systems to bring about change and development (James, 2002a, 2004; Murrel, 1986). OD and capacity building are delivered in various African countries by NGOs, external consultants, and internal consultants (James, 2002a).

A growing movement in Africa is influenced by the idealism of an African Renaissance. The antithesis of African pessimism, the African Renaissance urges Africans to "liberate themselves from colonial and post-colonial thinking and re-engage with an African value system" (Bolden & Kirk, 2009, p. 74). This process is also referred to as indigenization, defined earlier in this chapter. The convergence of African values with ideas imported from other places provides a progressive step but yet returns to the roots of African thought in management and change. Edoho (2001) argued that such effects are essential:

> Africa's effort to engineer authentic development will continue to be fruitless until endogenous management systems are established and firmly institutionalized. Management in sub-Saharan African countries must be conscious of the culture of the people, be appreciative of the societal value system and cosmology, as well as be purposeful in helping alleviate depressing poverty and menacing misery. (p. 4)

Table 2.1, adapted from Jackson (2004), traces an evolutionary development of African thought in management based on pivotal periods of African history. Jackson's table has four management orientations: postcolonial, postinstrumental, African Renaissance, and East Asian/Japanese. For this study, the table was modified by replacing postcolonial, postinstrumental, and East Asian/Japanese with the colonial management orientation. The characteristics of the colonial period were added for this study based on Casanova (1965). "This period was added because strong centralized governments inherited from the colonial period served well the original purpose of preserving law and order and enforcing taxation; it was not particularly well suited to the development needs of post-independence Africa" (Dia, 1996, pp. 36–37). The African Renaissance is a departure from the two preceding periods.

Summary

This chapter defined culture and discussed its importance in Africa. Culture was defined through leadership models that are prevalent in southern Africa today. Culture has been used to define and support some of the political systems in southern Africa. The chapter explored this notion in terms of the authoritarian regimes of Malawi's Dr. Banda and the Apartheid system in South Africa. Belief systems were explored within the context of understanding their role in advancing OD work. Proverbs and metaphors play an important role in illustrating the types of cultures that may exist in southern Africa. For instance, certain proverbs used in Malawi help to de-

TABLE 2.1 Developmental Stages of Management Practices in Sub-Saharan Africa

	Colonial	Postcolonial	African Renaissance
Main Principles	Theory X Western/preindependence European	Theory X Western/postindependence African	Humanistic Ubuntu Community Collectivism
Leadership	Predominantly White male	Authoritarian Predominantly elderly men	Democratic Gender sensitive and inclusive
Strategy	Divide and conquer Exploitation of cheap labor	Inputs and process orientation Lack of results and objectives Risk aversive	Stakeholder orientation
Governance and Decision Making	Authoritarian with native population Nonconsultative with native population	Authoritarian Nonconsultative	Participative, consensus seeking (pungwe, pabwalo, indaba, Lekogtla—large-group community interventions in South Africa and Malawi)
Character	Efficient Foreign owned Cheap labor Repressive toward natives Inequality	May not act ethically toward stakeholders Not very efficient Static Probably not foreign owned	Stakeholder interest may be more important than ethics Success related to development and well-being of its people Indigenous
Management Expertise	Elitist Educated with high managerial experience	Educated management elite with low managerial experience	Management expertise based on people orientation
People Orientation	Control orientation	Control orientation	People and stakeholder orientation
Management Motivators	Political Control Economic Military Spiritual	Economic security Control	Belonging Development of person and group

TABLE 2.1 Developmental Stages of Management Practices in Sub-Saharan Africa

	Colonial	Postcolonial	African Renaissance
Management Commitment	To home office To business objectives To organization	To business objectives To relatives To organization	To group To people
Management Principles	Theory X Repressive toward natives Racist	External locus of control Deontology Theory X Mistrust of human nature Status orientation	Internal and external locus of control Trust of human nature Status and achievement orientation
Management Practices	Reliance on hierarchy Divide and conquer Exploitation	Reliance on hierarchy Use of rank Low egalitarianism Lack of open communication Lack of open information	Participation Egalitarianism Communicating openly Providing open communication
Main Orientations	Managing power relations Production driven Profit making	Managing process Managing power relations	Managing people (internal stakeholder focus) Managing results (defined by stakeholder interests)

Source: Adapted from Jackson (2004)

fine its culture as being collectivistic. An opportunity exists for leveraging proverbs and storytelling in southern Africa for OD and change management. The chapter also defined the concept of indigenization as the key to successful applications of Western-developed OD techniques. The concept is utilized because it empowers African thought and voice in a field that is Western dominated. Finally, the chapter discussed Jackson's "African Renaissance" as an idealistic concept that aligns with the values of OD. The next chapter discusses the practical application of OD techniques in southern Africa and highlights the voices of practitioners who have worked with OD in southern Africa. It also explores the practical application of southern African-influenced techniques in the United States; specifically, the use of proverbs in models for planning is discussed.

References

Ali, S., Akuahmoah-Boateng, R., Bowa, M., Carr, S. C., Ehiobuche, I., Griff, P.... Zimba, C. (2001). Indigenising organizational change: Localisation in Tanzania and Malawi. *Journal of Managerial Psychology, 16*(1), 59–78.

Blunt, P. (1995). The cultural limits of process consulting in development assistance. In R. Reineke & R. Sulzer (Eds.), *Management consultancy in developing countries.* Berlin, Germany: Gabler.

Bolden, R., & Kirk, P. (2009). African leadership. *Le leadership Africain: L'apparition de nouvelles facultés de comprénsion grâce au développement du leadership, 9*(1), 69–86.

Casanova, P. G. (1965). Internal colonialism and national development. *Studies in Comparative International Development, 1*(4), 27–37.

Dia, M. (1996). *Africa's management in the 1990s and beyond: Reconciling indigenous and transplanted institutions.* Washington, DC: World Bank.

Dionne, S. D., Yammarino, F. J., Atwater, L. E., & Spangler, W. D. (2004). Transformational leadership and team performance. *Journal of Organizational Change Management, 17*(2), 177–193.

Edoho, F. (Ed.). (2001). *Management challenges for Africa in the twenty-first century: Theoretical and applied perspectives.* Westport, CT: Praeger.

García-Morales, V. J., Matías-Reche, F., & Hurtado-Torres, N. (2008). Influence of transformational leadership on organizational innovation and performance depending on the level of organizational learning in the pharmaceutical sector. *Journal of Organizational Change Management, 21*(2), 188–212.

Golembiewski, R. T. (1991). Organizational development in the Third World: Values, closeness of fit and culture-boundedness. *The International Journal of Human Resource Management, 2*(1), 39–53.

Hofstede, G. (1980). *Cultures consequences: International differences in work-related values.* Beverly Hills, CA: Sage.

Hofstede, G., & Hofstede, G. J. (2005). *Cultures and organizations: Software of the mind: Intercultural cooperation and its importance for survival.* New York, NY: McGraw-Hill.

Jackson, T. (2004). *Management and change in Africa: Cross-cultural perspective.* New York, NY: Routledge.

Jaeger, A. M. (1984a). The applicability of organization development overseas: Reality or myth? *Academy of Management Proceedings* (00650668).

Jaeger, A. M. (1984b). The appropriateness of organization development outside North America. *International Studies of Management & Organization, 14*(1), 23–35.

Jaeger, A. M. (1986).Organization development and national culture: Where's the fit? *Academy of Management Review, 11*(1), 178–190.

James, R. (2002a). *People and change: Exploring capacity building in Africa.* Oxford, England: INTRAC.

James, R. (2002b). What makes CSO coalitions effective? Lessons from Malawi. *INTRAC_Occasional Paper Series, 38,* 1–42.

James, R. (2004). Exploring OD in Africa: A response to David Lewis. *Nonprofit Management & Leadership, 14*(3), 313–324.

Jones, M., & Mann, P. (1983). Management development: An African perspective. In M. Jones & P. Mann (Eds.). *HRD: International perspectives on human resource development.* London, England: Kumarian.

Jones, M. L. (1989). Management development: An African focus. *International Studies of Management & Organization, 19*(1), 74–90.

Judge, T. A., & Piccolo, R. F. (2004). Transformational and transactional leadership: A meta-analytic test of their relative validity. *Journal of Applied Psychology, 89*(5), 755–768.

Malunga, C. (2009). *Understanding organizational leadership through Ubuntu.* London, England: Adonis & Abbey.

Masango, M. (2003). Leadership in the African context. *Ecumenical Review, 55*(4), 313–321.

Mbigi, L. (2000). Managing social capital. *Training & Development, 54*(1), 36–39.

Murrell, K. L. (1986). Africa and organization development: Is there any chance? *Organization Development Journal, 4*(1), 53–60.

Najafbagy, R. (1990). Culture and development in Third-World countries. *Organization Development Journal, 8*(4), 61–65.

Pillai, R., & Williams, E. A. (2004). Transformational leadership, self-efficacy, group cohesiveness, commitment, and performance. *Journal of Organizational Change Management, 17*(2), 144–159.

Swartz, E., & Davies, R. (1997). Ubuntu—The spirit of African transformation management—A review. *Leadership & Organization Development Journal, 18*(6), 290–294.

Thomas, A., & Bendixen, M. (2000). The management implications of ethnicity in South Africa. *Journal of International Business Studies, 31*(3), 507.

Vecchio, R. P., Justin, J. E., & Pearce, C. L. (2008). The utility of transactional and transformational leadership for predicting performance and satisfaction within a path-goal theory framework. *Journal of Occupational and Organizational Psychology, 81*(1), 71–82.

3

The Practice of OD and Africanism

If we have truly committed to follow our dream, we will find a powerful force exists beyond ourselves and our conscious will, a force that helps us along the way nurturing our quest and transformation.

—Joseph Jaworski

What are OD interventions? How do interventions facilitate the process of change and development? Interventions are planned activities used to improve organizational programmatic, individual, and team performance. OD is a process of change in an organization, therefore it should not involve someone coming in as an external consultant to offer an intervention for a couple of days and then claiming to have carried OD. For an organization to go through an OD process, its top leadership needs to recognize and accept that there are issues within the organization. An organization may have persistent challenges it has tried to resolve with other means unsuccessfully. The organization's leadership may see an opportunity to do more, to reposition, or to take advantage of new opportunities, while responding to threats in the environment. An organization would call a consultant to take them through an OD process. Typically, consultants will conduct an organizational assessment, identify a number of appropriate interventions, apply the interventions, and then evaluate them

Creating Opportunities for Change and OD in Southern Africa, pages 47–72

with feedback from the client. However much of what is happening in the name of OD is actually not OD.

There is a difference, however, between OD and interventions. A good OD process has interventions, but not all interventions are OD. A good OD process has interventions because OD is a process, and you can do those interventions in isolation at the request of the client; however, that does not necessarily mean that it is OD. Consultants are being asked to do more interventions other than OD. Some of the most common interventions in Africa are organizational assessments, project evaluation, leadership development, strategic thinking and planning, team building, board development, or restructuring of organizations (also called alignment). With the development of such interventions, one identifies a gap in the organization's current situation capacity, competency, and structure. As a result of the gap, the organization has to work to align its finances, skills, policies, culture, and values to the new strategy. On the other hand, in OD, the interventions build on existing culture and values.

The following are some types of interventions. These interventions are further defined with actual OD case studies applied in both Malawi and South Africa. The names of the organizations involved in these interventions have been changed to allow anonymity.

Coaching and Training Activities

Coaching is an individualized process that seeks to help leaders clarify their goals and objectives so that they can perform at their optimum level. The approach to coaching is usually done on a one-on-one basis; the consultant not only acts as a sounding board but also provides guidance, mentoring, and support to the leader. Coaching activities may be enhanced with training in areas where development is needed.

Case Study 1: Coaching and Training

This particular case study involves an NGO that worked with 53 HIV/AIDS-related Community Based Organizations (CBOs) on leadership development and mentoring in Malawi. Malawi, like the other countries in southern Africa, has a number of CBOs engaged in various activities. Some of the challenges these CBOs have had over the years are being led by leaders not experienced in community development. Some of these leaders, although committed to their organization's mission, have not possessed adequate knowledge, skills, and abilities to effectively run and manage an organization. Without effective leadership, CBOs are at risk of failure.

Approach

The following were the steps undertaken by the NGO to develop leaders of the CBOs:

- *Selection*: The consulting NGO developed criteria to select CBOs that were to participate in the mentoring and leadership development program.
- *Mentoring*: The leaders of the selected CBOs were partnered with a trained and experienced mentor for a 2-year period. The mentors visited their mentees on a regular basis, providing technical support and assistance using action learning wherein the leaders learned from their actions.
- *Training*: Comprehensive training was provided to cultivate a culture of learning and development.
- *Financial Support*: The CBOs were provided with experiential training on bookkeeping and budgeting. They were provided with a modest regular allowance while they developed their competencies in budgeting, tracking, and reporting. Full lump sums were then provided after they developed their competencies.

Results

The approach used by the NGO was a combination of both leadership and organization development. The experiential learning model ensured that as the leaders changed and developed, so did their organizations. This was replicated in other parts of Malawi.

Process Analysis Activities

Process consultation is an approach that helps with the improvement of interpersonal relationships, decision making, and performance. A consultant works with the client system to help them not only understand why something was done a certain way but guides them to improve based on what they learn from their actions.

Case Study 2: Process Analysis

This case study involved training in behavior modeling to address group interpersonal conflicts between White supervisors and their Black subordinates in two South African mines during Apartheid. At the time, workplace interracial relations were influenced to some extent by Apartheid's policies. In a situation in which there is tension and conflict that is racially charged, productivity is affected.

Approach

The following are the steps that were involved in the behavior modeling interventions:

- *Selection*: Both mines implemented behavior modeling programs with their White supervisors.
- *Questionnaires*: The White supervisors filled out questionnaires to assess supportive and abusive behaviors. The questionnaires were administered before the behavior modeling program 12 weeks after the training and then three months later.
- *Training*: The objective of the training was to provide White supervisors with appropriate interpersonal skills when working with their Black subordinates. The training thus involved the presentation of appropriate behavior, role-playing the appropriate behavior, and social reinforcement for those who correctly role-played the behavior.

Results

- Some 12 weeks after training, supervisors receiving behavior modeling training reported significantly greater improvements in supportive interpersonal behavior than did the untrained supervisors.
- Behavior modeling training enhanced self-reported supportive behavior.
- Behavior modeling training did not reduce the incidence of abusive supervisory behavior.

Team-Building Activities

Team building involves planned activities designed to enhance group cooperation and engagement for purposes of performing given tasks.

Case Study 3: Team Building

This case study took place at a local subsidiary of a multinational car manufacturer, where team-building activities were carried out to improve shop floor cooperation.

Approach

A team-based workshop that used process improvement tools was implemented. The team met extensively to diagnose the shop floor issues, develop an implementation plan, and monitor it. One of the issues the workshop addressed was that of a supplier who was delivering the wrong parts. The team was able to determine why this was occurring and addressed it.

Results

- The plant established an office to oversee the workshops with full-time personnel.
- Process improvements were valued at several million Rand per year.
- Participants of the workshops were able to appreciate and understand the roles of their teammates in the plant.
- The improvement workshops gained a lot of credibility because of the heavy emphasis and company support for getting team suggestions implemented.

Intergroup Activities

Intergroup activities are designed to build effective cooperation among groups. An example of this would be the cooperation between departments.

Case Study 4: Intergroup Activities

This case study is on a training program called the Training Development Scheme (TDS), which was designed to address racial and gender disparities in a metro area of South Africa. The program was launched during the transition from Apartheid to racial democracy. The goal of the program was to address the underrepresentation of persons of color in management positions of the local and provincial government.

Approach

The training supported the affirmative action program by developing the capacity of those who would be eligible to assume leadership and management positions. The training had the following components:

- *Internship*: This component allowed participants to have experiential training in various aspects of leadership, which included decision-making skills and management. Part of their internship involved formal lectures at the university, facilitation skills, and computer literacy.

- *Coursework*: The Training and Development Scheme had two formal training courses: a postgraduate diploma in public administration (with an emphasis on local government) and a certificate in development management.
- *Mentorship*: The training participants had support systems through mentorships. They were guided through an accelerated process of self-discovery, career growth, personal maturity, and job competence.

Results

- After one year, more than 60% of the trainees were employed by the council.
- A study tracing mobility of the trainees since the inception of the program revealed that approximately 70% of them have since been employed in local government.
- Research has also revealed that trainees from the council and province have enhanced the career development opportunities.

Implications of OD in Southern Africa

Successful organization development applications in cross-cultural settings are predicated on the ability of OD experts to adapt them to local conditions and context. Cultural frameworks have been utilized by global OD experts to understand the general cultural settings of environments in which they are working and applying OD techniques. However, the complexities of culture within organizations, communities, and countries may not always be understood within these cultural frameworks and models. Assumptions of culture based upon or reliant upon models alone can impede the successful applications of OD.

This section of the chapter discusses the role of cultural translation of OD within an African context. It examines the approach of Western consultants in an African environment as well as the approach of local African consultants as they interact with Western-developed OD applications in their own local environments. As part of my doctoral research, I conducted interviews with global OD experts based in the United States and the United Kingdom as well as local African OD experts based in Malawi and South Africa. The interviews that were held with global OD experts from both the

United Kingdom and the United States provided valuable insight on how important it is for external consultants to partner with local OD experts.

Cultural Translation of OD

A great challenge for OD in Africa concerns the need for contextualization or indigenization of OD applications for their effective and successful usage. There need to be cultural translations of OD applications in order for them to fit local settings. A local OD expert described this challenge as follows:

> I remember when we went to rural areas to work with CBO (Community Business Organizations); the first hiccup we had was language. How do you explain strategic planning to a grandmother in Nthenachena? How do you explain team building, concept of governance, process intervention? It was so difficult because the first place we went to practice OD was with a community-based organization. The conclusion we came up with was to say that principles of OD, like the principles of management in general, are universal, but the practice must be contextualized. For us, one of the things we had to contextualize was communication and language. Thus, when we came up with the issue of saying, "Well a village is a community, it is an organization." These people have been there for years; they must have some sort of organization. How do they manage themselves and where do we find that knowledge? We can come up with the idea of using indigenous wisdom contained in Africa proverbs, folktales, and indigenous concepts. By using that language, we can connect with the people. So we went to all the interventions we were doing at that time—strategic planning, team building, board development, developing structures, visioning—and tried to find what folktale, proverbs or indigenous concepts can we use so when we go the village and talk to people we will be talking the same language. We experimented with that, and it worked very well; and our work became more successful. We began to think this is something we can publish to share with others. Apart from what I am saying, I do not see much elsewhere where efforts are being very seriously to contextualize the language and concepts that I used. People are competing on what is the latest in terms of tools being used or concepts. As a professional, I have to keep myself abreast, but all the time the question I ask myself... balance score card. What does it look like? How do I communicate that to my people in a language they can understand? Actual learning cycle, how do I explain that in a language and concept that my own people can understand? I don't think there is much happening now in terms of contextualization. (Personal communication, October 22, 2010)

Indigenization of OD is thus not only about fitting the local setting but also about effectively communicating a process in a way that it is well understood by the recipients or clients. Cultural translation is both a language issue and a conceptual issue. The local OD expert cited above went on to state that there is a lack of resources to focus on cultural translations and learning because most local OD experts are busy with other work.

An American-based OD expert provided further insight into the role of cultural translation of OD in South Africa. She works with her clients in assessing their organization and then, based on her experience, proposes what she has identified as an appropriate intervention. However, her clients have the responsibility of ensuring that the proposed intervention is appropriate culturally as well as organizationally. She discussed the importance of indigenization when working with OD in Africa:

> I check with the clients. In other words, I will describe what I think might be an appropriate intervention, and then I will say how do we need to modify this to make it work for you? That approach has made me very successful not only in South Africa but in Ghana, Kenya, and other African countries because each one is slightly different, and anything that comes out of the United States has to be modified. It absolutely has to be modified. And when people think that they can go into another culture and think that what they do well here in the United States will work well there, they're being naïve. So, for me the easiest thing is to describe what I'd like to do and then say, "Okay, how do we have to change this to make it work here?" (Personal communication, December 8, 2010)

The challenge for African culture is that it has not been viewed as a contributor to management and development due to an embedded and historical colonial mentality from the West as well as the pessimism that has dominated Africa. The local OD expert acknowledged the following:

> But unfortunately from a historical point of view, African culture has not been given a chance to be utilized right from colonial times. When the colonialists came, they came with an agenda whereby everything African or local was looked at as backward, primitive, and a hindrance to development. As a result, in its place, let's put in Western civilization and values. African culture as such has not really been given the opportunity to make a contribution in significant terms to social change. Even now, when we talk about change, we always look to the West and to the North to glean the latest models and concepts about change. This is what we are struggling and dealing with in Africa. Nothing wrong with that because principles are universal, but the practice needs to be rooted in the local context. We have not really given African culture that opportunity to bring about real significant strategic change. (Personal communication, October 22, 2010)

One way to overcome this situation is "appreciative inquiry" (AI). According to Cooperrider, Sorensen, Yaeger, and Whitney (2005), "Appreciative Inquiry is a co-constructive inquiry process that searches for everything that gives life to organizations, communities and larger human systems when they are most alive, effective, creative and healthy in their interconnected ecology of relationships" (p. 6). AI offers a paradigm shift in the way we think and act. It is a shift from the deficit-based model of change, which focuses on problems and what ails us as individuals and organizations, to a positive and strengths-based model of change.

The American-based consultant cited above indicated that when she utilizes AI in South Africa, she first breaks away from the principal rule of focusing on strengths and instead begins with a process of catharsis, in which participants purge all the bad things that have happened. She argued that South Africans have to begin the process in this manner in order to be appreciative.

Partnering With Local OD Experts

The external OD practitioners I interviewed indicated that 95% to 100% of the time they are partnering with local OD experts because of their ability to accurately read local situations, whether cultural, political, or legal. One American consultant who has been involved in OD work in South Africa states,

> I never go into an organization without a local. I always have a cultural guide even if they are not part of the organization. So for example, when I was in Russia, I had friends who were Russian that I would tell them that I am observing this or that in a particular organization. Is that typical Russian behavior? Or is that atypical? So I always have somebody that I can bounce off what I am observing to make sure that I am making an accurate interpretation of the behavior because I don't know the behavior. (Personal communication, December 8, 2010)

Partnering with these local African OD practitioners helps to gain and build trust with the local workforce and organizations that are recipients of OD services. Relationships are important in an African setting, especially if they involve cross-cultural work. Local African talent is needed if the continent is going to become self-sustained. Global operations have tended to focus more on bringing in expatriates, with less recognition of existing local talent. It is interesting that most of the OD work occurring in Africa is done by NGOs as opposed to for-profit consulting firms.

Utilization of an African-Inspired Model in the West

The practice of using proverbs in OD is part of the indigenization effort that is helping organizations to culturally translate and understand Western-developed concepts in southern Africa. Chiku Malunga is one of the pioneers of using African proverbs and wisdom in strategic planning. In his 2009 book, *Making Strategic Plans Work: Insights from African Indigenous Wisdom,* he outlines how each step of strategic planning can be accomplished through the reflection of proverbs. He outlined the following four phases as part of the strategic planning process: preparation, formulation, implementation, and monitoring and evaluation.

Chapter 1 included a discussion of African thought and practice receiving limited attention in the West. This chapter will thus demonstrate the practicality of African concepts in a Western setting. This section of the chapter will introduce a planning model inspired by Malunga's (2009) approach to strategic planning using African proverbs and wisdom. The planning model will be described through actual Western-based case studies.

Introduction of the P8 Planning Process

The P8 Planning Process allows organizations to discover their collective wisdom through personal and group interpretation of proverbs. The model propels organizations to tap their wisdom from a deeper understanding of passion on a personal, group, and organizational level. This engagement model can be used for planning, leadership development, team building, process consultation, and evaluation. As shown in Figure 3.1, the model includes eight critical steps that are cyclical. Following the steps, proverbs from around the world can be used for reflection exercises as the organization goes through each phase.

The model is cyclical to denote the fact that planning is an ongoing process. The results of previous planning, which are evaluated in the eight steps, should feed into the first step of the planning process in the next round of planning.

Phase 1: Past

The purpose of this first step was to engage the group in developing a timeline of key events of the organization. The planning group would be asked to tell stories about significant events and their implications on the organization. This sharing serves as a foundation for the planning process. What are critical successes the organization could build upon for the fu-

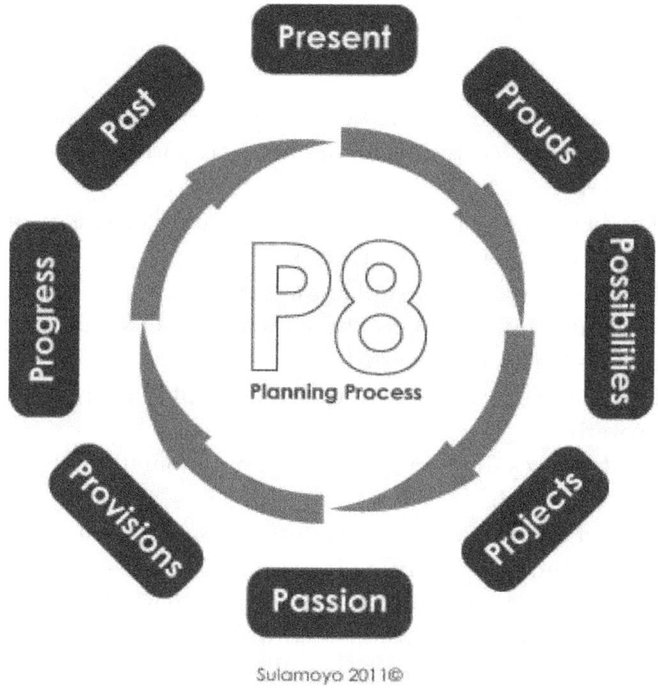

Figure 3.1 P8 Planning Process model.

ture? What are some of the failures and pitfalls to learn from? We have to know where we have been to know where we are going. How can the following proverbs, through reflection, help an organization to discuss the past?

- Sweet is the memory of past labor—Greek proverb
- A book is a good friend when it lays bare the errors of the past—Indian proverb
- The past is the future of the present—Japanese proverb
- Regretting the past is like chasing after the wind—Russian proverb

Phase 2: Present

The purpose of this second step is to mind-map the present by identifying trends and their implications on the organization. The result of this process is the scanning of the organization's internal and external environment. We have to know what is going on around us to know where we are going. How can the following proverbs help an organization to mind-map the present?

- Men see only the present; heaven sees the future—Chinese proverb
- All the past died yesterday; the future is born today—Chinese proverb
- The best time to plant a tree was 20 years ago. The second-best time is today—Chinese proverb
- If not today—when?—Indian proverb
- Too much hurry, and get there tomorrow; take time, get there today—Jamaican proverb
- Do today what you want to postpone until tomorrow—Lebanese proverb
- He that saves something today will have something tomorrow—Dutch proverb
- A good well-lived today makes every yesterday a dream of a good future, and every morning is a vision of hope—Sanskrit proverb
- Take a close look at today, because yesterday is but a dream and tomorrow is barely a vision—Sanskrit proverb
- Live today, for tomorrow it will all be history—Traditional proverb

Phase 3: Prouds

The purpose of this step is to acknowledge and to gain a shared understanding of the organization's internal capabilities. This step builds on the previous step by increasing confidence and energy for what could be accomplished by the organization in the future, given the state of its environment. How can an organization's strengths propel it into the future?

- Dwell not upon thy weariness, thy strength shall be according to the measure of thy desire—Arabian proverb
- If your strength is small, don't carry heavy burdens. If your words are worthless, don't give advice—Chinese proverb
- If thy strength will serve, go forward in the ranks; if not, stand still—Confucian proverb
- There is no strength without unity—Irish proverb

Phase 4: Possibilities

During this step of the process, the group discusses possibilities (opportunities) taken from the environment (external and internal) that the organization could address through strategic initiatives. What should the organization identify as opportunities for its future state?

- Opportunities come but do not linger—Nepalese proverb
- Our faults provide opportunities for others—Tamil proverb
- Opportunities neglected can never be recovered—Traditional proverb
- Hell is paved with good intentions, roofed in with lost opportunities—Portuguese proverb

Phase 5: Projects

This step involves the group's developing strategic initiatives or projects that would address some of the challenges identified during the environmental scan/discussion as well as possibilities identified for the organization.

- The rich man plans for tomorrow, the poor man for today—Chinese proverb
- The lazier a man is, the more he plans to do tomorrow—Norwegian proverb
- Last night I made a thousand plans, but this morning I went my old way—Chinese proverb

Phase 6: Passion

In this phase, the group prioritizes the initiatives they felt most passionate about for the organization to pursue. The prioritization is done democratically with each member of the group given a certain number of votes.

- I am the connections that I weave—African proverb
- The most useful holy war is the one fought against your own passions—Arabian proverb

Phase 7: Provisions

In this phase, the group identifies the resources needed to support the projects of the plan. These are not limited to money, personnel, supplies, and time.

- Eat according to the limits of your provisions; walk according to the length of your step—Tibetan proverb
- Lack of resource has hanged many a person—Irish proverb

Phase 8: Progress

In this final phase, the group discusses how they would measure success under each proposed strategic initiative. This phase evaluates the strategic plan.

- A foolish man may be known by six things: Anger without cause, speech without profit, change without progress, inquiry without object, putting trust in a stranger, and mistaking foes for friends—Saudi Arabian proverb

Case Study 1: Small Zoo Strategic Planning Process

The small zoo strategic plan was organically developed by a task force that was representative of the zoo's stakeholders and community representatives. The task force had no preconceived ideas or suggestions from which to work. The development occurred through a facilitated process that drew input from all members of the task force. The task force met over a period of 10 months to develop the zoo's strategic plan, collect data, and develop the strategies and projects of the master plan. This group of dedicated individuals gave personal time to develop a realistic plan for the zoo.

The task force used a strategic formulation and implementation approach referred to as the P8 Planning Process: Past, Present, Prouds, Possibilities, Projects, Passions, Provisions, and Progress. The methodology of the P8 Planning Process builds upon a more traditional SWOT (Strengths, Weaknesses, Opportunities, and Threats) strategic analysis to increase commitment and participation for a faster and more effective implementation.

The P8 Planning Process is an emerging framework that involves a strength-focused process of creating an organization's future. This framework allowed the zoo and its stakeholders to see where they were yesterday and where they are today and to establish a vision of where they want to go. It helped them to clearly identify, understand, and most importantly, communicate the people and organizational values, direction (vision), purpose (mission), core and unique capabilities (internal analysis), possibilities (external analysis), strategies and tactics, and structures and systems to create a positive organizational environment.

Phase 1: Past

The zoo did not have a recent strategic plan in place. The most recent planning document was the master plan that was developed in 1998.

Major exhibits—completed:

- Lemurs—1990
- Otters—1989
- Penguins—1987
- Australia Walkthrough—1999
- Cougars—1991
- Spider Monkeys—2000

Major exhibits—not completed:

- Tiger
- New Parking Area
- Bison
- Elk
- Snow Monkeys

Recent exhibits not included in the master plan:

- Asiatic black bear—Snow Monkeys
- Wolverine—American Black Bear
- Bobcat—Lynx
- Playground—Amphitheater

Phase 2: Present

Park District Background

- Large organization covering over 60 square miles
- 2,500 acres
- Two 18-hole golf courses
- Indoor and outdoor swimming facilities
- Over 37 parks

Park District Financial Information

- $7.5 million budget
- Issues bonds
- Receives grants

Park District Financial Challenges

- In 1996, there was a referendum on tax caps that limits levying abilities. This has an impact on growth.
- Tax cap limitation affects opportunities for growth.
- 60% of the budget's revenue is from tax levies.
- Revenue from receipts has been going down due to the economy.
- 40% of the budget is from other revenue-generating entities.

Phase 3: Prouds

The purpose of this phase was to acknowledge and to gain a shared understanding of the zoo's capabilities. This phase of the process sought to increase confidence and energy for what the zoo could accomplish in the future.

Below is a collective inventory of capabilities of the zoo:

- The passion of the zoo's staff
- The animal collection, such as the penguins
- Springfield residents and people from nearby communities have fond memories since childhood
- The zoo has a park-like setting
- The zoo offers fun programming
- Playground area is well used
- Picnic shelter is available for guests
- The zoo offers conservation projects and programs
- Zoo patrons are able to interact with the animals due to their ability to get close
- The zoo offers great volunteerism through the zoological society and other means
- The zoo offers uniqueness of exhibits
- Size of the zoo is ideal for families
- Resources are available from the park district to support the zoo
- The impact the zoo makes with the available animals—wolverine, breeding, etc.
- The zoo is handicap accessible
- The location of the zoo offers diversity of topography
- There is free and easy parking
- The zoo has supportive neighbors
- There is a genuine recognition of weaknesses and concerted effort to improve them
- The facility is open year round
- The gift shop and other attractions prolong the stay of a zoo visitor

Phase 4: Possibilities

The purpose of this phase was to develop organizational alignment with the external environment by recognizing opportunities among trends (state, national, and community), current challenges, what's changed and what hasn't, and how we should respond.

Below is a collective inventory of possible opportunities for the zoo:

- Get community involved and engaged in the zoo
- Enhancement of school outreach—animals can be taken to schools for educational purposes and programs
- The zoo could offer additional on-site education programming
- Meeting the animals and their zookeepers adopted by sponsors
- Creating a passport with other local museums—get a stamp at every place and want to see them all
- Increase the number of mixed-species exhibits
- Grow the number of interactive exhibits for children
- Bring in animals that connect with the public and draw people in
- Increase avenues for up-selling
- Change the exhibits to get new people visiting the zoo—rotate or change out exhibits
- Partner with other agencies to offer new exhibits
- Improve animal adoption program
- Foster partnerships through other events in the district
- Promote reciprocal agreements with other zoos
- Utilize volunteers to help with marketing
- Expand educational activities and volunteerism to higher education

Phase 5: Projects/Plans

The purpose of this phase was to develop specific projects and initiatives for the zoo. The group developed goals that were then synthesized into initiatives for the zoo. The zoo envisioned that the following strategies would serve as a guide in moving it toward successful accomplishments. These strategies and initiatives were developed from the intentional and candid conversations among the task force members participating in the strategic planning session.

Initiative 1: Branding/Marketing

- Goal 1: Bring to life a compelling and unified brand; build connections with the families in our community.
- Goal 2: Become a "regional class" destination.
- Goal 3: Establish a productive marketing program to the "whole package" offered by the zoo.
- Goal 4: Enhance awareness of native animals in the region covered/represented by the zoo.
- Goal 5: Build a customer service plan.

- Goal 6: Make Springfield excited about the zoo again.
- Goal 7: Provide a place where families want to gather and linger.
- Goal 8: Build a plan to expand the membership programs.

Initiative 2: Economic Development

- Goal 1: Create an endowment or savings for special projects.
- Goal 2: Find funding opportunities.
- Goal 3: Become financially self-sufficient.
- Goal 4: Build a fundraising plan that encompasses a money campaign, membership, endowment, and grant development.

Initiative 3: Educational Programming

- Goal 1: Develop curricula in conjunction with state standards for education; build awareness for all ages.
- Goal 2: Increase the educational options for people visiting the zoo.
- Goal 3: Grow the volunteer program.
- Goal 4: Improve our conservation impact—breeding, funding, release program—be the place to learn how to practice being "green."

Initiative 4: Expansion, Enhancement, and Improvement

- Goal 1: Enhance the exhibits' ability to utilize all of the topography—use the space we have.
- Goal 2: Develop a plan to create a welcoming, exciting, awesome environment—build the personal experience.
- Goal 3: Rebuild the structures so that they are inviting and welcoming to visitors.
- Goal 5: Build an exhibition plan.

Phase 6: Passion

The group decided to not prioritize the key initiatives identified. All of the initiatives were kept in the plan since only four were developed.

Phase 7: Provisions

The task force developed resources for the proposed projects and initiatives in subcommittees.

Phase 8: Progress

The purpose of this section was to determine how the zoo's desired outcomes were being achieved. Here the task force put together a list of indicators/measurements that were designed to serve as success factors indicating progress. This section sought to identify leading measures of desired strategic outcomes.

- Increase the number of organized school trips
- Develop 8–10 monthly outreach programs
- Increase retail sales
- Increase the number of partnerships created—higher education

Case Study 2: Strategic Planning for a Not-for-Profit Agency

The strategic plan for this not-for-profit organization, called "Vision 2010," had expired for several months. The Board of Directors and CEO of the organization requested the development of a new plan that involved the engagement of the agency's board of directors, policy council members, community partners, CEO's management team, and a staff focus group that consisted of a cross section of the agency's middle managers and intake staff.

The first phase of the planning process involved the review of the agency's preceding planning documents to this strategic plan and various program reviews/evaluations. This process was conducted by the consultants prior to the planning sessions with the agency's various constituent groups. Most particularly, the consultants reviewed the agency's plans of action developed for the various reviews that were conducted on the agency's key programs and services. This review served in part as the environmental scan and internal diagnosis of the agency.

This first phase of the planning process was designed to ensure a synthesis of the existing planning documents toward the development of a new strategic plan for the agency. The synthesis involved the identification of indicators and results to support accomplishments, the identification of unresolved challenges with their rationale, and the identification of aspirations and opportunities from the past planning processes that can support the design of the agency's future. This review essentially ensured that any unaccomplished tasks/plans/objectives would be addressed in the development of the 2015 plan, set the stage to build on the agency's and community's strengths, and utilized the information from the identified planning documents to mind-map the present. The review also identified the CEO's vision for the agency. Finally, the document review utilized the resultant information as the foundation for future visioning. The review was conducted from both the organization's and community's perspectives. It is critical for the organization to take inventory of its present capacity and opportunities for growth from these previous planning efforts and to position itself to deal with its community's needs effectively.

The second phase of the planning process involved the engagement of the agency's CEO management team and a staff focus group representing a cross section of the agency's staff, consisting of middle managers and intake staff. The groups were engaged separately in a strength-based model to develop strategic initiatives that the agency would work on in the next 3 years.

The third and final step was the engagement of the board of directors, policy council, and CEO through the same process. This final product is a synthesis of the three planning processes into one strategic planning document.

Phase 1: Past

The purpose of this first step was to engage the group in developing a timeline of key events of the agency. The group was asked to tell stories about significant events and their implications for the agency. This sharing served as a foundation for the planning process. What are critical successes the agency could build on for the future? What are some of the failures and pitfalls to learn from? We have to know where we have been to know where we are going.

- Establishment of corporate headquarters downtown was a perception changer for the agency as the organization was brought closer to corporate entities
- Establishment of sites in other areas that were not traditionally served by the agency
- Partnerships with faith-based organizations
- First food pantry started by the organization
- Emergency shelter started by the agency
- Scholarships offered to students

Phase 2: Present

The purpose of this second step was to mind-map the present by identifying trends and their implications on the agency. The result of this process is the scanning of the agency's internal and external environment. We have to know what is going on around us to know where we are going.

- Loss of staff leadership with skills, passion, and work ethic
- New staff coming into the organization need to have compassion and have practical knowledge of what the agency does
- Redefinition of the agency should not be solely dependent on government grants
- Economic development—agency spends funds in the community
- Space needs—more staff for the space available
- The rise in transportation costs
- Customers are changing—older, better educated, working poor, unemployed, and underemployed
- Needs are different today
- Government wants to look at nonprofits for efficiencies
- Funding cuts at state and national levels have affected employment because nonprofits are major employers
- Local businesses are closing
- Jobs that were assigned to seniors are now taken by young people who need jobs
- Educational needs and gaps, drug testing are affecting employability
- Resources that were a guarantee in the past are threatened
- Competition is disguised as collaboration
- There is duplication of efforts
- There is the issue of expectation versus reality on employment
- New generation of workers are not so service focused or driven
- Heads of households are getting younger

Phase 3: Prouds

The purpose of this step was to acknowledge and to gain a shared understanding of the agency's internal capabilities. This step built on the previous step by increasing confidence and energy for what could be accomplished by the agency in the future, given the state of the environment. The group was able to create a collective inventory of the agency's internal capabilities as follows:

- The agency has compassionate employees
- The internship program has tangible educational outcomes; two of the interns have not only completed their education but have also been hired by the agency

- The agency has programs that engage parents in decision making, such as through the policy council
- People helping people
- There is diverse leadership based on ethnicity, gender, educational background, social and economic backgrounds
- The organization is constantly growing; as needs change, the organization changes
- There is well-defined organizational leadership
- Community action has community visibility
- The organization serves as an information vessel with parents informing parents
- There is great board training and orientation

Phase 4: Possibilities

During this step of the process, the group discussed possibilities (opportunities) taken from the environment (external and internal) that the agency could address through strategic initiatives. The following is an inventory of possibilities that the group identified:

- Recruiting and training new staff to fill leadership positions currently vacant as a result of transitions.
- The agency could become the facilitator of a community training center that trains individuals with soft skills for entry or reentry into the workforce. The agency could assist in building a place and function as a bridge builder for customers to not feel intimidated. People fall through the cracks.
- The agency could explore the concept of business incubation, which was there in the 1980s. The businesses to be considered for this incubator would be those that address community service needs and skill development. The incubator could be utilized to develop skills for job readiness.
- The agency could explore franchise opportunities as a means of creating unrestricted funds for the organization and job creation through a fee-for-service structure. The agency could also explore a fee-for-service structure for some of its existing programs, such as weatherization and childcare.
- Addressing educational gaps in the community. There are many individuals without GEDs.
- Explore new partnerships.
- Creation of "green" projects that involve and engage the community, such as community gardening.

- Serving teenage mothers to improve the odds stacked against them. The agency could partner with other entities already serving this population.

Phase 5: Projects

This step involved the group developing strategic initiatives or projects that would address some of the challenges identified during the environmental scan/discussion as well as possibilities identified for the agency. These initiatives were also identified as a means to transition the agency from good to great.

- Initiative 1: Develop a program that provides assistance to single parents/teen mothers in the Head Start Program.
- Initiative 2: Create a foundation that will support the mission and vision of the agency.
- Initiative 3: Develop a public relations/marketing plan that is not event- or crisis-based and that utilizes multimedia tools, including social networking.
- Initiative 4: Create a community garden initiative.
- Initiative 5: Build a business incubator that provides training and business development opportunities to the community.
- Initiative 6: Identify resources to fund a housing development and management position.
- Initiative 7: Complete a facility and economic impact assessment.
- Initiative 8: Offer after-hours childcare for evening employees.
- Initiative 9: Pursue affordable housing development.
- Initiative 10: Collaborate with other agencies on job skills/match and employment readiness.
- Initiative 11: Assist former offenders with reentry into society.
- Initiative 12: Provide family support in the areas of transportation, budgeting, and drug rehabilitation.
- Initiative 13: Develop social networking communication tools for the agency.
- Initiative 14: Develop a Board and Policy Council mentoring program with a succession plan.

Phase 6: Passion

The group was asked to prioritize the initiatives they felt most passionate about for the agency to pursue. The prioritization was done democratically, with each member of the group allotted six votes. The following strategic initiatives emerged as the top of prioritized initiatives:

- Initiative 1: Develop a program that provides assistance to single parents/teen mothers in the Head Start Program.
- Initiative 2: Create a foundation that will support the mission and vision of the agency.
- Initiative 3: Develop a public relations/marketing plan that utilizes a multimedia approach.
- Initiative 4: Create a community garden initiative.
- Initiative 5: Build a business incubator that provides training and business development opportunities for the community.

Phase 7: Provisions

Provision or resources were identified in the implementation plan of the strategic plan.

Phase 8: Progress

The group discussed how they would measure success under each proposed strategic initiative. The following listings are indicators/measurements that should constitute success factors.

Initiative 1: Develop a Program that Provides Assistance to Single Parents/Teen Mothers in the Head Start Program

- Graduation and retention rates for selected teen moms will go up.
- Percentage of teen moms in the community will go down through preventative programs.
- Teen moms will be identified in high schools to boost GED attainment.
- Agency will target parents without their GEDs as addressed in the PIR.
- Teen parents will be prepared for work and go to college.
- Agency could assist teen parents with childcare as an incentive to get them back into school.

Initiative 2: Create a Foundation that Will Support the Mission and Vision of the Agency

- More unrestricted funding will be brought into the organization. The goal would be $250,000 to $500,000.
- Establish a 501(c)(3) (tax-exempt) charitable foundation
- Endowments from benefactors
- Agency will accomplish unfunded initiatives with nonfederal funding
- Creation of a foundation board
- More community visibility, with the ability to tell the story of poverty and community action
- More creative programming

Initiative 3: Develop a Public Relations/Marketing Plan that Utilizes a Multimedia Approach

- First timers applying for services
- More parental involvement
- More people want to get involved in the agency's services and activities because they get information
- Brand recognition in all three counties

Initiative 4: Create a Community Garden Initiative

- Total of nine community gardens throughout the agency's service areas
- Senior participation
- Youth participation
- Retention rates of participants
- Better time management by participants

Initiative 5: Build a Business Incubator that Provides Training and Business Development Opportunities

- Number of startups measured by how long they are sustained
- Pursue a franchise opportunity with new jobs for the community
- Influx of small business development
- Number of jobs created
- Unemployment goes down
- Public assistance recipients go down

Summary

This chapter defined interventions used in OD by illustrating them through case studies. The voices of local OD practitioners and those from the West who have worked in southern Africa provided insight to the approaches that work within that setting. They highlighted the importance of culturally translating Western-developed applications for their acceptance and effective usage by African organizations and communities. The second half of the chapter focused on demonstrating the applicability of African influenced approaches to OD in the West. It introduced the P8 Planning Process—influenced by Malunga's strategic planning model—which uses proverbs for reflection through each critical step of the process. The next chapter discusses the cultural models used to understand and explain culture in southern Africa.

References

Cooperrider, D. L., Sorensen, P. F., Yaeger, T. F., & Whitney, D. (Eds.). (2005). *Appreciative inquiry: Foundations in positive organization development.* Champaign, IL: Stipes.

Malunga, C. (2009). *Making strategic plans work: Insights from African indigenous wisdom.* London, England: Adonis & Abbey.

4

Cultural Models

For tomorrow belongs to the people who prepare for it today.
—African Proverb

Cultural models have been developed over the years to help us understand how to read, interpret, and understand culture. Culture is so complex and intrinsic that relying merely on cultural models, however, can lead to stereotyping cultural settings as opposed to appreciating their roles and values within society. The models discussed in this chapter are designed to provide us not only with an understanding of the influence of national culture but also with an appreciation of organizational culture. That is, national culture may have an influence on organizational culture, but organizations also have their own cultures.

Hofstede's Model for Understanding Culture

Hofstede (1980) and Hofstede and Hofstede (2005) developed four cultural dimensions that have been used by global OD experts to help determine the congruency of interventions with a nation's culture through organizations. These four cultural dimensions are as follows:

Creating Opportunities for Change and OD in Southern Africa, pages 73–93

- *Power Distance*: Low PD is associated with social egalitarianism, and as PD increases, status inequality and distance in social relationships also increase.
- *Uncertainty Avoidance*: Low UA is associated with tolerance of ambiguity and minimized structuring of relationships; high UA leads to elaboration of rules and structures.
- *Masculinity–Femininity*: The masculine polar type stresses results and the importance of material things, while its counterpart type stresses the importance of feelings and relationships.
- *Individualism–Collectivism*: Individualism stresses and tolerates individual uniqueness, while collectivism defines individuals through their social, group characteristics. (Johnson & Golembiewski, 1992)

Power distance and individualism-collectivism are discussed later in this chapter to define the culture of African organizations within the context of their national cultures. The countries of Malawi and South Africa will be used as models in this section to explain and understand Hofstede's model. Malawi has its cultural rankings analyzed along regional lines as part of East Africa, whereas South Africa is ranked on its own. Hofstede's cultural rankings did not cover all of the world's countries. According to Hofstede and Hofstede (2005), the scores for East Africa—which comprises Malawi, Kenya, and Tanzania—have the rankings listed in Table 4.1.

A review of the literature based on these countries' history, approach to governance, management, and usage of metaphors and proverbs suggests that prior to their new dispensations of government, East African nations had a high ranking of power distance (Fagenson-Eland, Ensher, & Burke 2004, p. 436). According to Balogun (2007), after gaining independence from their European colonial masters, many of the countries in Africa chose highly centralized administrative systems to support their authoritarian structures by centralizing power and control and thus quelling individual or group initiatives. Balogun described organizations in cultures

TABLE 4.1 Cultural Dimensions for East Africa

Cultural Dimension	Ranking
Power distance	64
Uncertainty avoidance	52
Masculinity	41
Individualism	27

high in power distance to be highly centralized with several layers of hierarchy. Both Malawi and South Africa have had authoritarian systems of government over a lengthy period of time, which consequently have had an impact on organizational management and behavior. According to Mbeta (2007), management and organizational literature shows that national culture affects organizational behavior (Hatch, 1997; Hofstede & Hofstede, 2005; Schein, Delisi, Kampas, & Sonduck, 2003). Mbeta argued in his dissertation, "Malawi's national culture influences its management behavior in light of the intercultural equilibrium model" (p. 55). He cited case studies and research by Jones (1988), Simon (1957), and James (2004) that support the hypothesis that national culture, as in the case of these countries, has had an impact on organizational behavior.

South Africa is a country with a rich culture and history. Although free of Apartheid, the future still holds many challenges. The nation and culture are in a state of transformation. The new dispensation of government, which is racially democratic, should have far-reaching effects on the culture and power structure. The majority of Black Africans, formerly excluded from positions of wealth and power by the White minority population, have increasingly expanding possibilities. As these individuals seize these opportunities, one could reasonably expect an alteration of business practices and cultural norms, and even a changed South Africa. Generalizing the South African culture proved to be a difficult task because the country has been racially democratic in only the past 16 years and is thus still in transition. However, due to decades of Apartheid, one can rationalize that for the purpose of business relationships, the White population's cultural tendencies remain dominant with regard to business practices. In a study conducted from 1967 to 1973, Hofstede surveyed and observed IBM employees in South Africa. One could reasonably conclude that such results would be heavily skewed toward the White population's attitudes and culture, which is why east Africa's cultural readings found in Table 4.1 are different from South Africa's cultural readings found in Table 4.2.

TABLE 4.2 Hofstede's Dimensions for South Africa

Cultural Dimensions	Ranking
Power distance	49
Uncertainty avoidance	49
Masculinity	63
Individualism	65

The non-White population of South Africa exhibits entirely different cultural characteristics. There is a propensity toward attitudes of collectivism. Supportiveness, cooperation, and solidarity sharply contrast with European values of individualism and tolerance for power distance. Currently, the characteristics of those with European heritage may represent the business culture more accurately, but that is rapidly changing (Prime, 1999).

Other Thoughts on Global OD

Yaeger, Head, and Sorensen (2006, p. 53) have used Hofstede's four cultural dimensions to determine how culture affects the applicability of OD interventions. The analysis the authors conducted ranks intervention methods based on what is limited by culture, what can be modified to fit culture, and what is universally applicable. These interventions were organized according to group orientation, technostructure, and total organization. Based on these groupings, only one intervention, the *t*-groups, was classified as being limited in its applicability because of culture. What is interesting for purposes of the adaptability argument made later in this chapter is that Yaeger et al. classified the rest of the interventions as adaptable to culture. However, the interventions were ranked differently if they were viewed from the context of development economics. Yaeger et al. (2006, p. 90) also classified the interventions based on undeveloped, developing, and developed economies. When analyzed in this context, the interventions have congruency issues according to the development setting. According to Yaeger et al., some interventions can be universally applied regardless of the development setting.

Another dimension used in assessing culture, particularly in a globalized world, is based on convergence or divergence among cultures. Convergence of cultures can be defined as a phenomenon wherein cultural diversity becomes less important with the goal of finding more commonality and shared values. In divergence of cultures, the focus is on diversity and separation, with emphasis on distinction of cultures. Yaeger et al. (2006) discussed how these two phenomena have affected global consulting in terms of understanding and defining how and why global OD can or cannot be successful. The authors identified scholars who have studied culture and have made the arguments for convergence or divergence. Hofstede's model, discussed in the previous section, is viewed from a divergent framework because it focuses on dimensions that distinguish culture at a national level. OD practitioners have used Hofstede's model to determine congruency with OD. How can we discuss or define globalization if there is a divergence of cultures? Is not convergence inherent in globalization? Should not culture be one of the variables that is used to measure how globalized we have become? Is there, as suggested by Yaeger et al. (2006, pp. 27–28), a middle ground that acknowledges convergence on an organizational level due to shared interests but divergence within the organization based on the diversity of the people? If global OD is limited by divergence of cultures, does it not risk being perceived as elitist? Should OD be practiced only in countries whose culture is convergent with the home country of the practitioner? How can OD help to transform the world through organizations if it is limited by the divergence argument?

Most of OD's approaches were developed in the West and are thus influenced by Western culture. According to Jaeger (1986), the appropriateness of OD techniques in non-Western cultures has been an ongoing challenge, and hence their introduction has met with little practical success. This situation seems to apply to religions such as Islam and Christianity, which were imbued with Western and Middle Eastern cultural influences and were brought to the continent of Africa. According to Odhiambo, "Europe moved in to fill Africa. It was to be a one-way traffic, with European philosophies, ontologies, epistemes, religions and metaphysics replacing the indigenous frameworks and systems of thought" (1997, p. 187). However, a cursory review of the success of religious influences in Africa demonstrates that their sustainability has been due to their Africanization at all levels.

Jaeger (1986) developed a model with OD values and national cultural values as the variables of congruency; his model analyzes OD values within the context of Hofstede's four-dimensional cultural model. According to Jaeger (p. 87), the OD values referenced earlier as democratic, optimistic, and humanistic when analyzed in the context of Hofstede's model, are rated as follows:

- Power distance: Low
- Uncertainty avoidance: Low
- Masculinity: Low
- Individualism: Medium

Jaeger's model was then used to determine congruency of OD with a nation's cultural values for purposes of interventions and the success of OD. He developed a rating system based on how different cultural values derive from OD values. This rating system showed only three countries aligned or congruent with OD values: Denmark, Sweden, and Norway. Of particular interest is the fact that the national values of the United States, according to Jaeger's model, are incongruent with OD values because they match on only two dimensions: masculinity-femininity and individualism-collectivism.

How is this possible when OD was essentially founded and developed in the United States? OD has flourished in this country and continues to be developed further at different levels. Why then is the exercise of matching cultural values to OD values important? Does it make a significant difference when global OD is a consideration? Even though Jaeger stated that OD had some difficulty being accepted in the United States (1986, p. 88), why has this movement been successful here with incongruent values to OD? Preston, Du Toit, van Zyl, and Holscher (1993) have characterized a majority of African cultures as being authoritarian. Does a perceived clash of this orientation with Jaeger's value model have an impact on congruency? Is Hofstede's or Jaeger's model relevant today if there is more of a convergence of cultures through globalization? What about the consideration for subcultures within the context of organizations? How do these models fit into that context? How does adaptability affect these models? These questions are important to put into perspective the argument for indigenization of OD in Africa.

The challenge that OD's presence has faced in Africa is based on its applications, which have often clashed with intrinsic African cultural values, making the sustainability of these applications short-lived. Jones (1989) is particularly clear about the problem:

> The training of African managers appears to have been designed to divorce them from the societies it is supposed to equip them to serve. Hofstede claims that Western management theories, although widely taught, are not practiced by non-Western managers. Successful managers perform a cultural transposition of ideas... there is no single formula for management development to be used in different cultures. (p. 79)

Criticisms of Hofstede and Consideration for Other Frameworks

Hofstede's model on the understanding of national culture has been criticized primarily for its methodology (Goodstein, 1981; Head, 1987; Hunt, 1981). The criticism is based on the fact that Hofstede's study was conducted within one multinational organization, raising questions of built-in biases. Hunt (1981) stated,

> There has been much formal and informal debate on the suitability of IBM employees as the target for his study on the breakdown of the massive sample (116,000) into country samples, on the dominance of male responses (especially in countries where females are not found in executive positions),

> on the built-in bias for the sort of people (are they minorities?) who are attracted to and selected by IBM as employees, on the use of a survey method to collect data and on the items from the survey used to collect data, and on the items from the survey used to establish the indices of difference. (p. 55)

Head criticized Hofstede's model by challenging the four assumptions underlying the model. The first assumption deals with the notion that citizens of the United States, as would those of any other country, have one set of values as defined in Hofstede's cultural dimension model. Head (1987) questioned the sample used by Hofstede to develop his cultural dimensions:

> While this is an impressive sample size, it only represents 12% of the original pool. What has happened to the other 88%? It is also interesting that the number of subjects from each country is not identified. These omissions must be taken with skepticism. For example using the only sample size identified (13,958), it can be established that the average number of subjects per country is 349. We are often asked to believe that 350 persons, all employed by the same company, may be used to classify an entire population's value set. This does not seem probable. (pp. 66–67)

Head's (1987) second argument against this first assumption is that there are more value sets than the four identified in Hofstede's model. He argued that there is no homogeneity when it comes to values. Indeed, he identified over 290 values, interests, and personality variables through review of organization behavior literature (p. 67).

Head (1987) also challenged the second assumption that the United States' management theories are aligned with its values. This assumption does not take into account the personal values of the theorist, which may or may not have anything to do with where the theorists come from or even the diversity within a culture.

The third assumption he challenged is that Hofstede's model is supported by the works of American organization behaviorists. Head contended that other fields of management, such as theory and strategy, have been influenced by non-Americans (1987, p. 67).

The fourth assumption Head challenged is that it is difficult for global OD experts to facilitate what this present study defines as indigenized OD, in which local values and culture converged with Western-developed methods. Head supported the notion that global OD experts learn to work through cultural differences and acknowledge the fact that each organization develops its own culture and value systems (1987, p. 68).

Practitioners' Response to Hofstede

Practitioners working in Africa find Hofstede's cultural model to be generally applicable. It provides a good framework for understanding culture. It does not, however, provide a full picture for understanding the intricacies of culture, particularly in societies that have multiple cultures, nor does it provide the framework for understanding organizational culture at the subcultural level of national culture. Practitioners understand the purpose of the model to be more culturally descriptive. It provides some initial impressions about what one might expect, but it doesn't play out as neatly as Hofstede describes it. Thus, the model provides practitioners with some guidelines to understanding the culture a little bit better or faster than travel guides, but it may not fully prepare one for actually dealing with the people. For instance, one may expect a male-dominated culture in South Africa but find that there are also women leaders in that culture.

Hofstede's model does not provide prescriptions when dealing with organizational issues within a cultural context. OD practitioners who rely solely on his model may develop preconceived notions about culture that are not always accurate and that may affect the successful application of OD interventions. Practitioners have to try to understand the client from the client's point of view. OD practitioners should assume that they are novices every time they work in a different culture. Assuming that they know and understand a culture based on a cultural model could lead to mistakes. If traveling through Malawi, one might conclude that Malawians are reserved or polite to a fault. This conclusion may be true in general, but it is not always true in every situation. Moreover, we must recognize that culture is dynamic. If Hofstede's model helps practitioners generally understand a particular cultural situation, then their challenges should be to discern organizationally how they may support the processes that are going well and the systems that are working well but also to determine how to confront those that are not. Each organization is different and develops its own culture. Of course the surrounding culture in which organizations are working influences, but organizations develop their own culture. Thus, Hofstede's conclusions are not the final word in understanding organizational culture. Practitioners have to do their own assessment in order to understand the culture they are working with. But at the same time, they should come back to the principles that state that the role of an OD practitioner is to support systems that are going well and to confront those that are not.

Binet's African Economic Psychology Model

Sub-Saharan Africa's cultural dimensions are complex because of the segmental cleavages of cultures and the cross-segmentation of cultures. This complexity limits Hofstede's cross-cultural theories in their understanding of cultural differences and interactions in Africa (Jackson, 2004, p. 37). James (2004) argued,

> While it is clear that there are some fundamental cross-cultural issues that must be taken into account to avoid the "bizarre attempts" to impose OD in another culture, it is dangerous to make sweeping generalizations about inherently dynamic national cultures, let alone continental cultures. There are usually significant regional or ethnic differences that make the situation much more complex. (p. 317)

Why are Africans not developing dimensions for understanding their own culture? Are there alternatives to Hofstede in Africa that have not emerged as acceptable models for understanding cross-cultural theories? Jackson (2004) and Hunt (1981) addressed these issues by acknowledging that even though Hofstede's model may have methodological issues, there may not be many other options in understanding national culture.

However, an earlier model developed by Binet (1970) does provide an African perspective to understanding culture and can be contemporized by Hofstede's model. Binet developed a model called the African Economic Psychology Model, which was the outcome of a study of 56 ethnic groups in Africa. According to Dia (1996), "Binet's findings show that African economic psychology is generally characterized by powerful connections between objects, human beings, and the supernatural, with the dominant guiding principle being the quest for equilibrium with both the supernatural and other human beings" (p. 54). Binet's model has five dimensions (see Table 4.3), which I have contemporized with Hofstede's model and Ubuntu by Mangaliso (2001).

Ubuntu as a Cultural Integrator of OD

Organization development (OD) is more than mere episodic interventions that bring about change and development in organizations. Jelinek and Litterer (1988) contend that OD has to be approached in the context of organizational strategy if organizations are to successfully manage change and sustain themselves in dynamic environments. This section explores the concept of Ubuntu as a cultural philosophy and way of life in southern Africa. Ubuntu represents southern Africa's humanistic way of defining life

TABLE 4.3 Cultural Models Applicable in Africa

Binet Dimension	Binet Description	Hofstede Dimension	Hofstede Description	Ubuntu
Sharing	Those who share their wealth in African societies can expect to be repaid in kind should the need ever arise	Femininity	Nurturing values of caring for others, security, good cooperation, and concern for the needy	Productivity: Must be optimized; solidarity and social harmony are important; rewards are shared, so is suffering
Commitment	The strength of commitments and contractual obligations in Africa resides in group pressure that springs from the associated formalism and rituals	Short-term orientation	Respect for tradition, fulfilling social obligations	Time: Not a finite commodity; it is a healer; allow enough of it for important issues before arriving at a decision
Compromise and Consensus	The traditional judge is more intent on reaching a consensus than in litigating by the book; Africans tend to seek unanimity	Uncertainty avoidance	The extent to which members of a society feel threatened by uncertain or unknown situations	Decision Making: Decisions by consensus; dissenters compensated for; process is circular; polyocular vision; dispute resolution to restore harmony
Congenial Social and Personal Relations	High value is placed on group solidarity and socializing	Collectivism	Definition of individuals through their social and group characteristics	Relationships with others: Relationships are reciprocal versus instrumental; treat others as your brother/sister; individual predicated on belonging to collective; "I belong therefore I am"; extended family is important
Deference to Rank	Hierarchy and deference between employer and employee is very important and within society; the marked subordination of younger members	Power distance	The extent to which less powerful members of society or organizations accept the unequal distribution of power	Age and Leadership: Age is an ongoing process of maturing and acquiring wisdom; older people are respected; grey hair is a sign of wisdom

Source: Adapted from Binet (1970), Hofstede (1980), Hofstede & Hofstede (2005), and Mangaliso (2001)

through others and hence is the key to effectively influencing strategies for change and development. According to Mangaliso (2001),

> *Ubuntu* can be defined as humaneness—a pervasive spirit of caring and community, harmony and hospitality, respect and responsiveness—that individuals and groups display for one another. Ubuntu is the foundation for the basic values that manifest themselves in the ways African people think and behave toward each other and everyone else they encounter. (p. 24)

The section also explores organizational culture and how that relates to perspectives of management and change. How is Ubuntu utilized as a cultural strategy for OD integration in Africa? How are OD and Ubuntu connected through basic values? How is Ubuntu integrated into African organizations as a means of facilitating change through a participatory approach? How do Western forms of strategy and change contrast with strategies imbued with cultural and indigenous relevancy? How does culture play a role in the facilitation of change in Africa? This chapter will discuss Ubuntu as a cultural integrator for OD in Africa. To understand Ubuntu in the context of organizational change and development, the chapter will also explore the African culture to provide the framework for understanding Ubuntu. The chapter concludes with an exploration of OD in the context of cross-cultural analysis and indigenization to understand Ubuntu from a global OD perspective.

The Role of Culture

Culture is an important aspect of understanding how countries, organizations, and managers behave. According to Mufune (2003), culture has four roles:

> 1. Culture shapes assumptions about what is important, useful, and relevant in organizations.
> 2. Culture helps to define individual interests thereby mediating the relationship between the individual and the organization.
> 3. Culture creates the rules for social interaction that conditions how people will react to others within the organization. Every form of interaction occurs according to rules (norms) of what is the appropriate form of communication according to gender, age, social status, kinship etc.
> 4. Culture shapes processes of power—how it is distributed and legitimated within organizations. (pp. 25–26)

Ubuntu

If OD is to be hybridized successfully or indigenized in southern Africa, a framework is needed that serves as a cultural integrator. In this case, that framework is Africa's philosophy of Ubuntu. Desmond Tutu (1999) defined Ubuntu thusly:

> *Ubuntu* is very difficult to render into a Western language. It speaks of the very essence of being human. When we want to give high praise to someone we say, "Yu, u nobuntu", "Hey, he or she has *ubuntu*." This means they are generous, hospitable, friendly, caring, and compassionate. They share what they have. It also means my humanity is caught up, is inextricably bound up, in theirs. We belong in a bundle of life. (pp. 34–35)

Ubuntu can be part of the strategy for converging Western-developed OD interventions with African culture to affect successful change and development strategies. Culture as an integration strategy is justified in Africa because Ubuntu espouses a way of life that, if not taken into consideration, would clash with the Western thought of change and management.

Ubuntu and OD Strategy

What does this all mean in terms of OD strategy? How is Ubuntu used to integrate the cultural differences that may exist within OD interventions developed in the West? In this section, OD strategies developed from OD interventions by Jelinek and Litterer (1988) are discussed and compared. The objective is to determine whether cultural integration can occur within OD strategy in southern Africa (see Table 4.4).

To understand Ubuntu as a strategic cultural integrator of OD, the OD interventions identified by Jelinek and Litterer (1988) were matched to the assumptions of Ubuntu developed by Mangaliso (2001). Seven strategies are examined.

Group Process (OD) vs. Relationship With Others (Ubuntu)

OD's approach utilizes group processes to accomplish a strategic need. Ubuntu, on the other hand, focuses more on the relationship of the group, believing that if people feel valued, they contribute more toward the thrust of the organization. The philosophy of "I am because we are" denotes a strong sense of empathy that the group values.

TABLE 4.4 Integrating Factors of Ubuntu and Organization Development Strategy

Assumption[a]	Ubuntu[a]	OD[b]	Strategy[b]	Ubuntu Competitive Advantages[a]	Strategic OD[b]
Relationships with others	Relationships are reciprocal vs. instrumental; treat others as your brother/sister; individual predicated on belonging to collective; "I belong therefore I am." "Extended family is important"	Group process	Developing products and market strategies	People are intrinsically motivated to contribute more when they are valued members; mutual respect and empathy are Ubuntu advantages	Using group processes to develop robust designs for products reflecting not only manufacturing and marketing but changing strategic needs
Language and communication	Oral tradition; to name is to create; meaning of words strongly related to context; poetic expression and ability to play with words are signs of wisdom	Sociotechnical focus on work teams	Technology selection	Shared understanding of deeper meanings supports complex consensus; Ubuntu communication means concerted action that is adaptable	Broad organizational and systems designs to link activities and team across the organization
Decision making	Decisions by consensus; dissenters compensated for; process is circular; polyocular vision; dispute resolution to restore harmony	Group decision making	Strategic planning	Ubuntu might be slow to action, but greater commitment to goals means more long-term effectiveness	Facilitating coalitions to envision and create new strategic potential
Time	Not a finite commodity; it is a healer; allow enough of it for important issues before arriving at a decision	Managing organizational change	Identifying new products for market opportunities	Punctuality is a virtue, but time's healing dimension is a hidden competitive advantage for Ubuntu	Helping managers craft new strategic organizational paradigms

(continued)

TABLE 4.4 Integrating Factors of Ubuntu and Organization Development Strategy (continued)

Assumption[a]	Ubuntu[a]	OD[b]	Strategy[b]	Ubuntu Competitive Advantages[a]	Strategic OD[b]
Productivity	Must be optimized; solidarity, social harmony important; rewards are shared, so is suffering	Designing jobs for individuals	Creating organization designs appropriate to technology and market demands	Sustainable competitive advantage comes from strong loyalty to group goals in Ubuntu	Creating a climate to foster information sharing and new definitions of managerial roles and power
Age and leadership	Age is an ongoing process of maturing and acquiring wisdom; older people are respected; grey hair is a sign of wisdom	Team building, socialization	Analysis of merger potential	Older workers bring experience, wisdom, connections, informal networks, competitive advantage from Ubuntu	Making cultural adaptation among merged units effective
Belief systems	Belief in the Creator, uNkulunkulu, and the existence of the mesocosmos; the mediating role of the isangoma; Christianity is now prevalent	Helping teams cope with stress	Setting achievable goals	Spirituality brings out the best qualities in humans; Ubuntu has the edge	Recognizing performance pressure and facilitating new technology and structure to achieve vast improvements humanely

[a] Mangaliso (2001)
[b] Jelinek & Litterer (1988)

Designing Jobs for Individuals (OD) vs. Productivity (Ubuntu)

In OD, the art of designing jobs for individuals takes into consideration the alignment of systems, behavior, culture, and organizational structure for purposes of the organizational strategy. Ubuntu, on the other hand, focuses more on loyalty, solidarity, social harmony and sharing of rewards, and suffering as the strategy for productivity.

Team Building Socialization (OD) vs. Age and Leadership (Ubuntu)

Team building in OD is about cultural adaptation, as, for example, in an environment of a merger. If the merger were to be conducted within the philosophy of Ubuntu, in order for socialization of the team to take place, age and experience would have to prevail.

Group Decision Making (OD) vs. Decision Making (Ubuntu)

Group decision making in OD is about strategic planning and facilitating coalitions to create change. In Ubuntu, decision making is about consensus, which results in longer term commitment to the change.

Managing Organizational Change (OD) vs. Time (Ubuntu)

In OD, managing organizational change is about the development of new organizational paradigms. Time is a critical element for Ubuntu, in which more time is allowed for any important decisions to be made.

Helping Teams Cope With Stress (OD) vs. Belief Systems (Ubuntu)

Managing stress for purposes of achieving organizational goals humanely is critical in OD. Belief systems in Ubuntu bring about the best qualities in humans. As discussed in the previous chapter, belief systems and spirituality are important components of African culture.

Sociotechnical Focus on Work Teams (OD) vs. Language and Communication (Ubuntu)

In OD, the selection of technology can facilitate system design that links the organizational team. In Ubuntu, the meaning of words leads to a deeper understanding of complex issues. According to Karsten and Illa (2005), "*Ubuntu* does not only enhance communication between management and employees but provides voice too, i.e., a participatory interaction where openly conflictual social formation can occur, producing voice and inventive ways of living together" (p. 609).

It is important to discuss OD strategy within the context of Ubuntu in southern Africa because of the challenges and opportunities that exist there for change. If OD can facilitate change within organizations and communities, then there is an opportunity for transformational change to occur. Southern Africa is indeed multidimensional politically, economically, culturally, and socially; however, other characteristics, such as the collectivist view of society, define the continent along some commonalities. Ubuntu offers itself as a southern Africa philosophy that can act as a cultural integrator of OD applications developed in the West that can be indigenized and hybridized for successful implementation. If OD is to grow globally, then adaptability will need to be added to its classic values of democracy, optimism, and humanism.

Noncultural Models and Frameworks

As the organization development movement takes root in southern Africa, background and contextual factors need to be taken into consideration by OD professionals intending to work in that region. The collectivist culture that permeates most of southern Africa was discussed earlier as a major factor for OD professionals to be cognizant of when they are working in that environment. However, culture is not the only factor. OD professionals also need to be aware of other key factors so that they can successfully bring change in an environment that others have inaccurately portrayed as pessimistic and inhospitable to OD. These factors need to be discussed and understood in the context of alignment with OD values and opportunities for change and development in sub-Saharan Africa.

Yaeger et al. (2006) offered other frameworks besides Hofstede's cultural model to be considered when examining the congruency of OD and management practices in global settings:

> Culture is critical, for it presents issues that govern how a particular intervention should be implemented. However, a nation's level of economic development is even more fundamental. As will be seen, economic factors will determine the driving forces behind organization development, such as: Is there a problem? Are the problem's costs significant enough to warrant attention? Is the solution likely to be more expensive than the problem? Which interventions will work given the nation's related conditions? (p. 81)

Yaeger et al. (2006) explored the congruency of OD interventions with economic conditions attributed to countries based on their gross domestic product. They suggested that OD scholars should consider the legal model when dealing with global OD. Their discussion of this framework was based primarily on how laws, such as employment laws, of a particular country could affect the application of an intervention.

Other fields of management, such as strategy and risk assessment, have developed more comprehensive methods of assessing organizational environments that could be applied to global OD for congruency. For example, Gillespie (2007), Evans and Richardson (2007), Forbes, Smith, and Horner (2008), and Walsh (2005) discussed the PESTEL model, which is more extensive in its consideration of the implementation of management practices through an assessment of the environment. According to Gillespie (2007), the PESTEL model identifies political, economic, social, technological, environmental, and legal factors when determining congruency with management practices or in assessing risk.

OD professionals should borrow from this environmental scanning framework to analyze the environments of a particular country in southern Africa for purposes of alignment and indigenization of OD applications. Before this analysis is done, one must understand the history of African countries, particularly their colonial history, because it may provide some context for understanding the results of the PESTEL analysis. All the countries in southern Africa were at one time colonized by a European country. After these countries gained independence, most became autocratic, and some are now pseudodemocracies. Clearly the legacies of their colonial, postcolonial, and now pseudodemocratic experience have influenced the social, legal, economic, political, and technological development in this region. Many of these countries are in transition, facing new changes and challenges.

The following questions should aid in analyzing this region. What role does OD have in countries that are in transition? How does OD adapt and indigenize to the environment described after a social, legal, economic, political, and technological (SLEPT) analysis has been conducted? How can OD contribute not only to change within organizations but also to large-system changes at a national level? How does a PESTEL analysis, which provides macro-environmental reports, reflect organizations at a micro-environmental level?

An OD professional should understand how social factors play a role in the subcultural context of organizations in Africa. Some of the social factors impact how segmental cleavages defined along tribal, racial, and ethnic lines may influence the climate and structure of certain organizations. In South Africa, for instance, for many years the Apartheid system was designed to place White South Africans in positions of power and deny Black South Africans the opportunity to hold those positions. It is important to understand the legacy of that system because of how it may influence organizational culture and, to some extent, organizational structure today. In other places, such as Malawi, there have been assertions that positions of power are being held by people who belong to the president's tribe. These assertions have created consternation among those Malawians who do not belong to that particular tribal or ethnic group. Understanding the intricacies of this complex and dominant issue in most parts of the African continent should be a prerequisite before any OD work is done because of the implications it has organizationally. Obviously, many other social factors must be considered when doing OD in Africa. However, OD professionals should be looking for opportunities to align OD or indigenize OD so that those factors are not hindrances but enablers for change and development. For example, there are gender issues in which OD could play the role of providing the vehicle for empowerment within organizations and the community at-large. The following are a few social factor questions OD professionals should ask: Can OD play a role in addressing the various segmental cleavages found in Africa organizationally? How can OD facilitate the building of effective teams when working with groups that perhaps have had a history of conflict? What OD strategies would be effective in engaging communities in change when they have high illiteracy rates? How does the HIV/AIDS pandemic affect organizations? How does one conduct effective leadership development?

Politics, political systems, and political environments play important roles in Africa. These factors have some influence on the culture and climate of organizations because they also affect the legal and economic dimensions. Again, this area requires astuteness and sophistication. In some countries, it could mean a life and death situation or a legal situation if OD work is perceived to be in conflict with the power structure. The following are some of the questions OD professionals should address when looking at the political environment: How does one deal with engagement if the organizations exist within a political system that does not accept openness or even criticism? How does corruption impact effective change within organizations? What role can OD play in facilitating large-system changes? What lessons can southern Africa learn about large-system change from its northern Africa counterparts who were democratizing in 2011? Can OD play a role in that type of change?

Indeed, many opportunities for OD exist in southern Africa, particularly its alignment with the potential for an *African Renaissance* as described by Terence Jackson in his 2004 book *Management and Change in Africa.* The *African Renaissance* promotes the humanistic, democratic, and optimistic values of OD. With an understanding of the PESTEL factors, OD can succeed in Africa through indigenization without compromising these values. Arguably, in some instances, OD work may be risky. But OD professionals who strive to understand African countries from the perspective of Africans—given the complexities of culture, politics, social structures, economics, technology, and legalities—will find that this movement can find acceptance in all sectors of organizations in southern Africa.

Summary

This chapter discussed three models for understanding and interpreting culture. Hofstede's cultural model is perhaps the most influential in the field of OD. Practitioners have acknowledged its value in understanding broad cultural descriptors of national culture. However, the model does not provide a means for understanding segmental cleavages that may exist within national cultures. Critical reviews of the model are discussed in the chapter. The chapter offers African-based cultural models as alternatives to Hofstede's model. The collectivist approach, which is encapsulated in Ubuntu, was discussed within the context of strategic OD and the cultural integration of OD in southern Africa. The voices of both local and global OD practitioners were important in gaining further insight into the applicability of cultural models when working with OD techniques. The next chapter takes a scholarly approach to measuring the successes of OD interventions in Malawi.

References

Balogun, M. J. (2007). The nature and effectiveness of training for decentralised administrative systems in Africa. *International Journal of Public Sector Management, 1*(1), 51–64.

Binet, J. (1970). *Psychologie economique Africaine.* Paris, France: Payot.

Dia, M. (1996). *Africa's management in the 1990s and beyond: Reconciling indigenous and transplanted institutions.* Washington, DC: World Bank.

Evans, C., & Richardson, M. (2007). Assessing the environment. *Manager: British Journal of Administrative Management, 60*(Oct/Nov), i–iii.

Fagenson-Eland, E., Ensher, E. A., & Burke, W. W. (2004). Organization development and change interventions: A seven-nation comparison. *Journal of Applied Behavioral Science, 40*(4), 432–464.

Forbes, D., Smith, S., & Horner, M. (2008). Tools for selecting appropriate risk management techniques in the built environment. *Construction Management & Economics, 26*(11), 1241–1250.

Gillespie, A. (2007). *Foundations of economics.* Oxford, England: Oxford University Press.

Goodstein, L. D. (1981). Commentary: Do American theories apply abroad? *Organizational Dynamics, 10*(1), 49–54.

Hatch, M. (1997). *Organizational theory: Modern symbolic and post modern perspectives.* New York, NY: Oxford University Press.

Head, T. C. (1987). International organization development: A case of cultural blinders or tinted sunglasses. *Organization Development Journal, 5*(4), 66–69.

Hofstede, G. (1980). *Cultures consequences: International differences in work-related values.* Beverly Hills, CA: Sage.

Hofstede, G., & Hofstede, G. J. (2005). *Cultures and organizations: Software of the mind: Intercultural cooperation and its importance for survival.* New York, NY: McGraw-Hill.

Hunt, J. W. (1981). Commentary: Do American theories apply abroad? *Organizational Dynamics, 10*(1), 55–62.

Jackson, T. (2004). *Management and change in Africa: Cross-cultural perspective.* New York, NY: Routledge.

Jaeger, A. M. (1986).Organization development and national culture: Where's the fit? *Academy of Management Review, 11*(1), 178–190.

James, R. (2004). Exploring OD in Africa: A response to David Lewis. *Nonprofit Management & Leadership, 14*(3), 313–324.

Jelinek, M., & Litterer, J. A. (1988). Why OD must become strategic. *Research in Organizational Change and Development, 2,* 158–162.

Johnson, K. R., & Golembiewski, R. T. (1992). National culture in organization development: A conceptual and empirical analysis. *International Journal of Human Resource Management, 3*(1), 71–84.

Jones, M. (1988). Managerial thinking: An African perspective. *Journal of Management Studies, 25*(5), 481–505.

Jones, M. L. (1989). Management development: An African focus. *International Studies of Management & Organization, 19*(1), 74–90.

Karsten, L., & Illa, H. (2005). Ubuntu as a key African management concept: Contextual background and practical insights for knowledge application. *Journal of Managerial Psychology, 20*(7), 606–620.

Mangaliso, M. P. (2001). Building competitive advantage from Ubuntu: Management lessons from South Africa. *Academy of Management Executive, 15*(3), 23–33.

Mbeta, P. (2007). *The effect of national culture on management behavioral norms in Malawi.* (Dissertation, Benedictine University, Ann Arbor, MI.) UMI Number: 3254825.

Mufune, P. (2003). African culture and managerial behavior: Clarifying the connections. *South African Journal of Business Management, 34*(3), 17–28.

Odhiambo, A. (1997). African perspectives on cultural diversity and multiculturalism. *Journal of Asian & African Studies (Brill), 32*(3/4), 185.

Preston, J. C., Du Toit, L., van Zyl, D. E., & Holscher, F. (1993). Endemic violence in South Africa: An OD solution applied to two education settings. *International Journal of Public Administration, 16*(11), 1767–1791.

Prime, N. (1999). *Cross-cultural management in South Africa: Problems, obstacles, and agenda for companies.* Proceedings of the seventh Cross-Cultural Consumer and Business Studies Research Conference, Cancun, Mexico.

Schein, E. H., DeLisi, P. S., Kampas, P. J., & Sonduck, M. M. (2003). *DEC is dead, long live DEC: The lasting legacy of Digital Equipment Corporation.* San Francisco, CA: Berrett-Koehler.

Simon, H. A. (1957). *Administrative behavior: A study of decision-making process in administrative organization* (2nd ed.). New York, NY: McMillan.

Tutu, D. (1999). *No future without forgiveness.* London, England: Rider.

Walsh, P. R. (2005). Dealing with the uncertainties of environmental change by adding scenario planning to the strategy reformulation equation. *Management Decision, 43*(1), 113–122.

Yaeger, T. F., Head, T. C., & Sorensen, P. F. (2006). *Global organization development: Managing unprecedented change.* Greenwich, CT: Information Age.

5

Meta-Analysis of OD Case Studies from Malawi

I am personally convinced that one person can be a change catalyst, a "transformer" in any situation, any organization. Such an individual is yeast that can leaven an entire loaf. It requires vision, initiative, patience, respect, persistence, courage, and faith to be a transforming leader.

—Stephen R. Covey

Why is it important to measure and evaluate the success of OD interventions? How has OD been evaluated for success by OD scholars? What would be the appropriate method or model for measuring success rates of OD interventions in southern Africa? What are the different schools of thought on measuring success of OD interventions? Much has been invested in the application of OD and capacity building, but less has been reported on the successes of the planned interventions. According to James (2002a),

> While considerable resources are being invested in capacity building prescriptions, we often avoid the rigorous examination of the outcomes. We need to analyze capacity building outcomes in much more depth to find out whether or not our interventions are effective and to explore the condi-

Creating Opportunities for Change and OD in Southern Africa, pages 95–113

> tions that contribute to their successes. This is certainly a very difficult and complex process. (p. 2)

James (1998) cited both methodological and practical problems in evaluating the success of OD in Africa. Methodological problems dealt with defining OD consulting and the effectiveness of OD interventions. The other methodological problems he identified had to do with the subjectivity of the success of an intervention. The question here was whether one could attribute organizational effectiveness to the success of an intervention or if other factors applied. James brought up issues of instrumentation, access, and research bias:

> The need for control or experimental groups is very difficult in OD field research. Just as with this research, organizations involved in OD self-select themselves making random assignment almost impossible. Furthermore, there are very real issues about who will conduct the research and how external they can be. Too close involvement with OD can lead to suggestions of consultant bias; too distant involvement raises very real problems of access. (pp. 138–139)

Finally, Jackson (2004) acknowledged that empirical research in the field of management in Africa overall has been lacking. Most of the data available has been descriptive.

The field of OD has had to deal with scientific challenges about the validity of measurements used to determine the effectiveness of its interventions (Johnson, Head, & Sorensen, 1989; Vicars & Hartke, 1984; Woodman & Sherwood, 1980; Woodman & Wayne, 1985). These challenges have been raised because the methodologies utilized in the past for evaluations have been subjective and without established scientific basis.

> The quality of studies assessing the effectiveness of OD interventions has been questioned for many years. Too many of these evaluations have provided only anecdotal information, and the criteria for success have been too subjective and testimonial in nature. When systematic evaluations have been attempted, for the most part they have had serious methodological weaknesses: Limited use of control groups, focus on short-term changes, and lack of independent evaluations are three in particular that have been complained about frequently by OD critics. (Vicars & Hartke, 1984)

This chapter examines success factors of organization development in Malawi over a 16-year period. This examination is done through the extrapolation of a meta-analysis conducted on OD applications from Malawi and South Africa (Sulamoyo, 2011). The time frame for the study was from

1994 to 2010, a critical time for both countries as they transitioned from authoritarian regimes to more democratic regimes.

Even though southern Africa is diverse in its political environment, economic structures, and social and cultural background, there are common and shared characteristics (Jones, 1988). Malawi and South Africa were selected as models because of these commonalities, as well as because of the contrasts they offered, representing countries in southern Africa. The original meta-analysis thus involved 38 case studies from South African and 27 case studies from Malawi. However, the results discussed in this chapter will be representative of only Malawi's case studies. This approach supports the argument made by Bullock (1986):

> The basic unit of research in OD is a case study. If we accept the fundamental assumption that organizations are complex social systems composed of interrelated subsystems, then the simplest possible unit of research for understanding social systems is not a laboratory study of individuals or even field study comparing work groups, but rather a case study in which the organization is viewed as an intact, integrated whole. This suggests that a case study is in fact the most important single unit of analysis for understanding the impact of organization development. (p. 33)

The OD cases were actual interventions conducted in organizations by OD consultants in Malawi and studies of actual cases by scholars. The study utilized Golembiewski's models for the measurement of success rates in OD. Golembiewski's (1994) model has four rating dimensions: highly positive and intended effects, definite balance of positive and intended effects, no appreciable effect, and negative effects.

Research Objectives

The discussion of the research in this chapter offers the following objectives: The first objective is to advance Golembiewski's (1982, 1994) work by discussing OD success rates in Malawi. Golembiewski (2010) admitted to not covering much of Africa in his previous studies. This study supports his previous findings by determining high OD success rates in southern Africa similar to what he found in other developing settings.

The second objective is to contribute knowledge to the limited literature on OD in Africa, particularly southern Africa. This discussion on OD success rates aims to serve as the antithesis to the African pessimism, which has focused on the negative aspects of the continent of Africa and not enough on the successes in management, development, and change.

The third and final objective is to discuss the development of consulting model for Malawi. According to Kerber and Buono (2009),

> Companies in every industry are increasingly challenged to build a capacity for change, both in response to and in anticipation of continuously changing competitive, market and technological pressures. Given this need, significant attention has been devoted to conceptualizing and empirically testing a range of change management practices. Much of this effort, however, has focused on how to best implement specific organizational changes. While this emphasis has improved the ability of organizations to deal with the myriad ramifications of a particular change, many of these models and prescriptions continue to fall short of the challenge. (p. 69)

Overview of Methodology

The focus of the research reported in this chapter involves a meta-analysis of change management and OD case studies from Malawi between 1994 and 2010. The meta-analysis was conducted through an evaluation of the case studies by an independent panel of OD experts. The methodology for the study was a meta-analysis for OD case studies as described by Bullock (1986). The meta-analysis comprised the following steps:

1. Literature search
2. Set study criteria
3. Develop research questions
4. Develop subject and keyword search
5. Collect case studies
6. Profile case studies
7. Develop the coding scheme
8. Rate the case studies
9. Assess reliability
10. Resolve discrepancies in ratings
11. Report results
12. Review threats to validity and reliability
13. Develop model and theory

The study used Golembiewski's (1982, 1994) model for evaluating OD case studies in the meta-analysis. Golembiewski's model served as the coding scheme for the meta-analysis. The following are Golembiewski's rating dimensions for the meta-analysis:

- Highly positive and intended effects—assignments required a substantial proportion of large changes due to OD intervention—that is, either statistically significant changes at the .05 level or changes greater than 10%–15% when statistical procedures were not employed—as well as few or no negative changes in the 30-plus variables on which intended changes were expected.
- Definite balance of positive and intended effects—assignments reflected a smaller proportion of large intended changes.
- No appreciable effects.
- Negative effects—assignments went to cases with negative differences in pre-test vs. post-test observations, some of these being quite large. (1991, p. 42)

Research Questions

The following research questions are addressed when discussing the results for Malawi's OD interventions:

1. How can OD success and management be understood in a context in which there may be a clash between Western-developed applications with African cultural, economic, political, and legal dimensions?
2. To what extent are African traditional values a part of OD and management processes in southern Africa?
3. How does the congruency of OD values and national culture contribute to the success of OD interventions? Is there a correlation between the types of OD interventions in Malawi and the *Ubuntu* philosophy?
4. How can results from evaluating OD case studies in Malawi contribute to the development of a more comprehensive and applicable OD model in southern Africa?
5. What are the relationships between the types of OD applied in Malawi with organizational settings and the system levels of interventions?
6. What impact do system levels and settings for Malawi have on success rates?
7. What is the effect of applied OD interventions for Malawi on success rates?

Research Variables

Independent Variables

Case Study Characteristics

- Type of OD intervention (diagnostic, process analysis, system building, team building, intergroup, technostructural, skill building, coaching/counseling, strategic planning activities)
- System level involved (individual, group, organizational)
- Setting (public, not-for-profit, profit, and community)

Dependent Variables

Golembiewski Rating Factors

- Highly positive and intended effects
- Definite balance of positive and intended effects
- No appreciable effects
- Negative effects

Research Assumptions

Two research assumptions are considered when discussing Malawi's results. The first is that Malawi has cultural, economic, and political attributes that are representative of southern Africa. This is a big assumption in that it does not take into account or dwell on the segmental cleavages that may exist within these two countries. What the assumption does is focus on the general characteristics of the selected two countries, such as national culture, the economy, colonial history, and postcolonial history as a representation of the characteristics of southern Africa. Jones (1988) provides support for this assumption: "Although artificially divided into over 40 politically independent nations, and encompassing a wealth of religions, traditions and ethnic groupings, there are in what is usually called Black Africa a number of shared socio-cultural characteristics" (p. 481). This assumption also was influenced by the following factors:

- *Factor 1*: OD in Malawi reflects the cultural dimensions defined by Binet (1970), Ubuntu, and some of the rankings from Hofstede's model (Hofstede 1980; Hofstede & Hofstede, 2005).
- *Factor 2*: OD successes in Malawi are more prevalent in the group and organizational settings than in the individual setting.

- *Factor 3*: The success rates of OD in Malawi are representative of OD success rates in southern Africa.
- *Factor 4*: There are fewer individual-level OD interventions in Malawi because of the collectivist culture prevalent in other southern African countries.

The second assumption in this meta-analysis was that Western-developed management and OD applications are unsustainable unless they converge with local culture. Further, if OD applications are applied with Western cultural orientations, they will clash with African or local culture, and success rates will be low. This assumption is supported by the earlier discussions of indigenization, which is the process that leads to the convergence of Western-developed OD interventions with local African culture. Moreover, the assumption is supported by the recognition of indigenously developed OD interventions, which need to have their place in the catalog of OD interventions. There also needs to be recognition of OD work that is succeeding in Africa but may be regarded as unorthodox by Western scholars. Three factors underlie this assumption:

- *Factor 1*: When OD is a product of local knowledge and culture, it will be successful within that context.
- *Factor 2*: A model for OD interventions can be developed for Malawi utilizing Ubuntu as the framework.
- *Factor 3*: When OD is not a product of local culture and knowledge, it will not be successful.

The meta-analysis involved identification of OD interventions prevalent in Malawi and their measurement for success utilizing Golembiewski's rating factors (Golembiewski, 1982, 1994; Golembiewski, Proehl, & Sink, 1982;). Contrary to arguments made by Blunt (1995) and by Jones and Mann (1983) that Africa is inhospitable to the successful application of OD, the results of the study showed that success rates are high in Malawi. This finding validates Golembiewski's findings that success rates are generally high when OD practitioners make necessary adjustments to their interventions to fit local cultures (Golembiewski, 1991, 1994; Golembiewski et al., 1982). In a recent interview, Golembiewski (2010) stated,

> Roughly speaking without making any distinctions, the success rates in every country that we looked at was in the 75% plus range. Most people and many prominent ODers among them thought this was apple pie in the sky. But as we added cases, there seemed to be a reasonable reflection of what existed in the world. Now why that should have been a surprise I can't un-

> derstand, because there were at that time in the 80s and early 90s approximately 20 or 30 small scale success rate studies that already existed. And they were uniformly positive. So that if people were reading that literature they should have been aware that at least if you did not make a methodological insistence on large populations there was something there. And when there is smoke, there is fire. Well we began developing fairly substantial populations in North America for example. It was over 500 cases, and they revealed approximately the same tendencies. Substantial success rates in the 75% plus range that did not vary very much when the populations got bigger. (pp. 2–3)

Assessing the Reliability Pre- and Postconference

Since there were four different dimensions for measuring the success rates of OD interventions, and three different raters, it was necessary to assess interrater reliability. According to Bullock (1986), "The most useful measure for inter-rater reliability is the simple measure of percent agreement, calculated as the proportion of identical ratings" (p. 40). Since there were three raters assessing the case studies, the statistic was calculated for each rater and then computed for the entire set by basing it on the proportion of what the three independent raters had as common ratings. Bullock stated that the percentage of agreement determined under this section of the analysis should be utilized in resolving discrepancies among the raters on all four dimensions.

For the present study, interrater reliability and agreement were measured in two ways. The first reliability measurement was calculated based on how the three raters ranked the 27 Malawian case studies independently. The reliability was calculated by adding the number of case studies in which the raters had agreement divided by the total number of case studies. In case studies in which the raters had disagreement, the reliability was determined by assessing how far apart the raters were among the four dimensions.

The second reliability measurement was calculated after the raters held a conference to share results and discuss discrepancies, a process covered in the next section. The present study chose to calculate it based on pre- and postconference to ensure that the criteria for measurement were clearly understood by each rater.

Resolving Discrepancies in Ratings

A conference to resolve discrepancies in how the case studies were rated by the three independent raters was critical in developing consensus. This conference helped resolve any errors based on a mislabeling of the case studies or a transposing that could occur given the number of case studies that were part of this present study. The rating challenge could have been based on what was perceived as success and what was not. How do African's perceive success? Is that different from the Western perception, particularly in OD? Most of the case studies for this study were presented in a research format as opposed to anecdotal. This had been the case even for those studies that were not obtained from publications. Only a few case studies were anecdotal, minimizing discrepancies that would be a product of interpretation.

The raters met after assigning the numeric values to each one of the case studies. Each rater provided a score for a case study, and these were recorded on a sheet of paper. As the raters shared their results, the case studies for which there was no agreement were identified and set aside to be revisited during a discussion. Each rater provided a rationale for rating the case study. They went back to either the spreadsheet or the actual case study to support their rating. If a case study was rated a 2 instead of a 1, the raters had to demonstrate why the case study should have been rated a 1, and that method was applied to all of the rankings. Golembiewski's (1982, 1994) criteria were revisited to ensure that the raters were abiding by the rules of resolving discrepancies. For each case study in which there was no agreement, there was discussion based on the criteria and the results of the case study. In some instances, the raters misread the results and, after discussion and a review of the case study itself, agreed on one ranking.

Results of the Meta-Analysis

The results of the meta-analysis are presented as descriptive statistics. The dataset for Malawi is analyzed to gain an understanding of when successful OD is occurring.

Types of OD Interventions Within Settings for Malawi

There were no interventions in the for-profit sector for Malawi's case studies in the meta-analysis. In the not-for-profit sector, strategic planning activities were the leading intervention, at 26%; the least prevalent intervention in the not-for-profit sector was team-building activities, at 0%. In the public sector, technostructural activities were the only intervention (100%). This particular case study involved the decentralization of local assemblies in Malawi as part of its enhancement of democratic values within its new dispensation of government. This process had mixed results in that decentralization had led to abuse of public resources and corruption. In the community sector, technostructural and skill-building activities were the only interventions, at 50% each. The skill-building activities in this sector involved an action research approach for linking smallholder farmers to markets. Specifically, the intervention activities involved fostering community-based capacity for the inclusion of rural women and the poor in analyzing and accessing market opportunities. The approach had great results, with farmers' abilities changing significantly. The results also showed that technostructural activities were the most common, comprising 100% in the public sector and 50% in the community sectors. Strategic planning and skill-building activities were the leading interventions, at 22%. The least prevalent interventions in Malawi within settings were team-building activities, at 0%.

Types of OD Interventions Within System Levels for Malawi

This section discusses the types of OD interventions for Malawi within system levels. In the individual level, skill-building activities were the only intervention, at 100%. In the group level, skill-building activities were the leading intervention, at 40%; the least prevalent interventions were process analysis, system building, team building, coaching/counseling, and strategic planning activities, which had no representation (0%). In the organization level, strategic planning activities were the leading intervention, at 32%; the least prevalent interventions were team-building activities, with no representation (0%).The results showed that skill-building activities were commonly prevalent in the individual and group system levels.

Rating Factors Within System Levels for Malawi

This section shows how the interventions in the three system levels were rated by the rating factors for Malawi. The group level had 60% of the interventions rated as successful, while 40% of the interventions within the group level were rated as failures. The individual level had 66% of its interventions rated as successful, while 34% of its interventions were rated as failures. The organization level had 74% of its interventions rated as successful, while 26% were rated as failures. Interventions for the system-level category were analyzed based on the total number of interventions for Malawi. The system level with the most successful interventions was the organization level, with a 51% success rate. The group level was second, with an 11% success rate. The individual level had an 8% success rate. The organization level had a higher failure rate, 18%, than did the other two levels. The group level had a failure rate of 8%, and the individual level had a failure rate of

4%. The results showed that 70% of the interventions were successful, while 30% were not successful.

Rating Factors Within Settings for Malawi

This section shows the results of the meta-analysis classified by settings for Malawi. The interventions within the community level for Malawi had a 100% success rate, whereas the for-profit sector had no representation (0%). The not-for-profit setting had a 69% success rate and a 31% failure rate. The public setting had a success rate of 50% and failure rate of 50%. The setting with the most successful interventions was the not-for-profit setting, with a 59% success rate. The community setting was second, with a 7% success rate. The for-profit setting had no representation. The public setting had a 4% success rate. The not-for-profit setting had the highest failure rate of 26%, followed by the public setting at 4%.

Types of OD With Rating Factors for Malawi

Skill-building activities and strategic planning were the most successful types of OD in Malawi, with success rates of 27%. The least successful types of OD were diagnostic, intergroup, and technostructural activities, with failure rates of 24%.

Discussion of the Results

This section answers the questions, "How does the congruency of OD values and national culture contribute to the success of OD interventions?" and "Is there a correlation between the types of OD interventions in Malawi and the philosophy?" Chapter 4 presented the cultural models of Binet (1970), Hofstede (1980), Hofstede and Hofstede (2005), and the Ubuntu model of Mangaliso (2001). The analysis of the results for Malawi was conducted through a comparison of interventions most common across settings and systems in terms of prevalence and success. These interventions were then compared with cultural models through the definition of the interventions and cultural factors for the model.

Systems and Culture

The data for Malawi was extrapolated from the meta-analysis. When the data from Malawi was analyzed, the organization level had the highest success rates, followed by the group level and individual level. The results

TABLE 5.1 Cultural Dimensions Congruent to System Levels

Binet Dimension	Binet Description	Hofstede Dimension	Hofstede Description	Ubuntu
Congenial Social and Personal Relations	High value is placed on group solidarity and socializing	Collectivism	Definition of individuals through their social and group characteristics	Relationships with others: relationships are reciprocal vs. instrumental; treat others as your brother/sister; individual predicated on belonging to collective; "I belong therefore, I am"; extended family is important

Source: Adapted from Binet (1970), Hofstede (1980), Hofstede & Hofstede, (2005), and Mangaliso (2001)

of this analysis were congruent with the following cultural variables and factors, as shown in Table 5.1.

Specifically, the organization and group levels were representative of Binet's (1970) dimension, which focused on group solidarity; Hofstede (1980) as well as Hofstede and Hofstede's (2005) collectivism dimension; and Ubuntu's collectivism dimension. The results from Malawi's dataset indicated that the individual levels were less emphasized. The individual level had a success rate of only 8% for Malawi. The present study argues that this level of the organization had such a low success rate in Malawi because it clashed with the culture, which is predominantly collectivist, as illustrated in Table 5.1.

Themes of Interventions in Malawi

Skill building emerged not only as one of the most prevalent interventions across systems and settings for Malawi's dataset but also as a common intervention that had a high success rate. Golembiewski (1982) defined skill building as "various designs for gaining facility with behaviors consistent with OD values, as in giving/receiving feedback, listening, resolving conflict, etc." (p. 89). The present study characterized activities that

TABLE 5.2 Cultural Dimensions Congruent to Type of OD

Binet Dimension	Binet Description	Hofstede Dimension	Hofstede Description	Ubuntu
Sharing	Those who share their wealth in African societies can expect to be repaid in kind should the need ever arise	Femininity	Nurturing values of caring for others, security, good cooperation, and concern for the needy	*Productivity:* Must be optimized; solidarity, social harmony important; rewards are shared, so is suffering

involved capacity building and knowledge exchange as skill building. The definition of this type of intervention is congruent with the following dimensions from the three cultural models: Binet, Hofstede, and Ubuntu (Table 5.2).

Capacity building and knowledge exchange were congruent with Binet's (1970) dimension of sharing, Hofstede (1980) as well as Hofstede and Hofstede's (2005) femininity, and Ubuntu's dimension of productivity. The purposes of the case studies utilized for this meta-analysis supported the congruency with the dimensions found in Table 5.2. Malawi had case studies that dealt with how organizations coped with the HIV/AIDS pandemic, which has affected the workforce in that country and, in particular, how organizations can change their culture, structure, policies, and procedures with a workforce and clients affected by HIV/AIDS. This is congruent to Hofstede's (1980) as well as Hofstede and Hofstede's (2005) femininity dimension, which promotes caring for the needy and others.

On the other hand, 89% of Malawi's case studies dealt with capacity building and the development of civil society and NGOs. This finding indicated Malawi's new dispensation of government, which was in transition during the time frame selected for the study. Malawi transitioned from an authoritarian regime, in which the role of civil society was greatly diminished, to participatory democracy, in which civil society has flourished. As discussed earlier, capacity building is congruent with Binet's (1970) dimension on sharing. Capacity building involves the sharing of knowledge.

Method for Developing a Consulting Model

This section answers the question, "How can results from evaluating OD case studies and empirical studies in Malawi contribute to the development of a more comprehensive and applicable OD model in southern Africa?" The proposed method for developing a consulting model for Malawi was to be based on cases that represented leading OD interventions within settings and system levels for Malawi compared to the types of OD interventions with the highest success rates from Malawi. It was not possible to develop a consulting model because prevalence did not always match high success rates.

Implications of the Study

The present study provides practical implications for organization development and change in organizations from Malawi. This section discusses five implications.

Prevalence Versus Success Rates

The present study identified skill building in Malawi as one of the most prevalent or most frequently utilized intervention. Skill building also emerged as an intervention with one of the highest success rates. However, the correlation between prevalence and success rates did not always apply. The present study identified other interventions that were frequently utilized but did not necessarily have the highest success rates. In the dataset for Malawi, for example, technostructural activities were identified as one of the prevalent interventions, equal to skill building, but it had the lowest success rate.

Success Rates in Systems

Malawi ranked the organization level as having the highest success rates, followed by group and individual levels. These results are supported by the collectivist cultural setting prevalent in Malawi.

Success Rates in Settings

In Malawi, the not-for-profit sector had the highest success rate. This could be based on the fact that Malawi's economy is perhaps not as industrialized compared to other economies in southern Africa. Malawi's economy has been mainly agrarian driven, with 90% of its labor force employed in the agriculture sector and 10% in industry and services. Malawi's Growth Domestic Product (GDP) official exchange rate was estimated at $5.673 billion in 2011. The GDP composition has been agriculture (30.3%), industry

(16.7%), and services (53.0%) (https://www.cia.gov/library/publications/the-world-factbook/geos/mi.html).

Measuring Indigenized OD

It was difficult to identify types of OD that had been indigenized in their applications from those that had not been indigenized. This situation also made it difficult to assume that interventions that had the lowest success rates had not been indigenized. The meta-analysis ended up focusing on the interventions in general without distinguishing between what was indigenized and what was not indigenized. There is an assumption, however, that OD practitioners used reasonable judgment to modify applications to fit the local culture and the political and economic environment. This assumption was addressed by triangulating the results of the meta-analysis with interviews conducted with OD practitioners. They provided insight as to how their interventions were indigenized to fit the local settings for successful applications. As discussed earlier, these practitioners were selected because of their OD experiences in southern Africa and because they had case studies, which are included in the meta-analysis.

Success Rates

Success rates for Malawi's dataset supported Golembiewski's (1982, 1991, 1994, 2010) results from measuring OD success rates in developing settings. Malawi had a success rate of 70%.

Limitations of the Study

The results of this study present great challenges for generalizing southern Africa when segmental cleavages characterize national cultures. This challenge supports the fact that OD practitioners have to continue to make reasonable adjustments and accommodation to their interventions if they are seeking high success rates. Relying on cultural models that generalize very diverse cultures can lead to lower success rates if reasonable accommodations are not made. Malawi may be representative of countries in English-speaking southern Africa, however, developing a single model for the region may not be possible given the heterogeneous culture of that part of the continent.

The meta-analysis has four major limitations:

- A meta-analysis is dependent on the findings of other studies. This can be limiting in that whatever is reported by the principal investigators of the case studies has to be accepted in the meta-analysis. The principal investigators determine descriptions of success or failure, which could bring into question issues of consistency for the meta-analysis.
- The publications and case study reports used for the present study were all in English. A search did not include OD case studies from Malawi presented in other languages, such as Chichewa, Chitumbuka, or Chilomwe.
- The types of OD interventions, system levels, and settings identified for the case studies could be debatable. They were assigned based on interpretations of the narrative contained within the case study and matching that with Cummings and Worley's (2005, p. 148) definitions of OD interventions and Golembiewski's (1991) definition of the types of OD he utilized in his studies.
- The results of the meta-analysis discussed in this chapter reference only one country. This could have been limiting because Malawi does not represent a sample diverse enough to cover all of southern Africa.

Recommendations for Future Studies

Even though the present study is built on Golembiewski's (1982, 1991, 1994) work, it has opened up more opportunities for OD research in southern Africa. The results of the study have indicated that OD success rates in Malawi are very high. However, as discussed earlier, it was difficult to discern how exactly culture played a role in the indigenization of the case studies included in this meta-analysis. An assumption has been made on the cultural modifications of OD interventions.

There are four recommendations for future studies. The first recommendation would be to conduct the meta-analysis regionally in Africa. This approach would provide the study with more robust data, which is representative of more than the country presented in the study. Selecting countries to represent southern Africa would not only deal with cultural differences, but it would also deal with some of the economic, political, and social issues that describe the environment for OD's application in Africa.

The second recommendation would be to survey all principal consultants on the case studies that would be included in the meta-analysis. The purpose of surveying them would be to obtain more specific data for the meta-analysis. For instance, the profiling of the case studies would be done with the assistance from the data obtained in the survey. This would ensure that there would be no misclassifications of the types of OD. Surveying the principal consultants would also address the assumption of whether indigenization or modification was part of their approach. If indigenization was part of their approach, then the questions would be as follows: What considerations were made? Were they political, cultural, or economical?

The third recommendation would be to collect indigenous work that has contributed to OD within organizations and communities of Africa. This collection of legitimate indigenous OD work would allow OD practitioners in Africa to take the next step of having their work recognized as part of the field. This work would also be part of a meta-analysis that investigates OD case studies from different regions of Africa.

The fourth and final recommendation would be the utilization of an African-based model on measurements of success as well as models such as Golembiewski's (1982, 1991, 1994) that were developed in the West. Two sets of independent raters would be used for the meta-analysis. The first set would be from Africa and the second set would be from the West. The purpose of designing the meta-analysis in this manner would be to investigate if there are any different perceptions for success that are culturally influenced. The independent raters would rate the case studies twice, utilizing each model. The purpose of the meta-analysis would be to compare the results of the study. This comparison would also address the issue of whether or not Western-developed models are always culturally sensitive when applied elsewhere.

It is important to discuss OD within the context of Africa because of the challenges and opportunities that exist there for change. If OD can facilitate change within organizations and communities, then there is an opportunity for transformational change to occur in Africa, particularly southern Africa. Africa is indeed multidimensional politically, economically, culturally, and socially. However, some characteristics define the continent along some commonalities, such as the collectivist view of society. This cultural commonality allowed for this research on OD in Africa to be conducted through the two selected countries as microcosmic models of southern Africa.

Summary

This chapter used an academic approach to measure the success of OD interventions in Malawi. The approach was a meta-analysis of 27 OD case studies from Malawi. The chapter discussed the types of interventions that are successful in Malawi as well as where these successes are occurring within organizations and types of organizational settings. A model based on prevalence and success of OD interventions is proposed for Malawi. This meta-analysis suggests that the major findings extend beyond academic objectives. OD practitioners can utilize the results of this study effectively to apply OD interventions within the context of generally acceptable cultural frameworks that define and consider subculture and segmental cleavages. The present study provides hope to southern Africa that change is a highly successful concept, particularly when it carries with it the values of OD, which are defined through democratic, optimistic, and humanistic principles. The next and final chapter builds on the successes of the meta-analysis by discussing opportunities for OD in southern Africa. This discussion is based on trends, observations, and experiences. Different models are proposed for OD interventions in southern Africa.

References

Binet, J. (1970). *Psychologie economique Africaine.* Paris, France: Payot.

Blunt, P. (1995). The cultural limits of process consulting in development assistance. In R. Reineke & R. Sulzer (Eds.), *Management consultancy in developing countries.* Berlin, Germany: Gabler.

Bullock, R. J. (1986). A meta-analysis method for OD case studies. *Group & Organization Studies, 11*(1/2), 33–48.

Cummings, T. G., & Worley, C. G. (2005). *Organization development and change* (8th ed.). Mason, OH: Thomson South-Western.

Golembiewski, R. T. (1991). Organizational development in the Third World: Values, closeness of fit and culture-boundedness. *The International Journal of Human Resource Management, 2*(1), 39–53.

Golembiewski, R. T. (1994). OD applications in developmental settings: An addendum about success rates. *International Journal of Organizational Analysis (1993–2002), 2*(3), 295–308.

Golembiewski, R. T. (2010). Building beyond already established OD success rates: An interview by Dalitso Sulamoyo. *Organization Development Journal, 28*(4), 11–19.

Golembiewski, R. T., Proehl, C. W. Jr., & Sink, D. (1982). Estimating the success of OD applications. *Training & Development Journal, 36*(4), 86–95.

Hofstede, G. (1980). *Cultures consequences: International differences in work-related values.* Beverly Hills, CA: Sage.

Hofstede, G., & Hofstede, G. J. (2005). *Cultures and organizations: Software of the mind: Intercultural cooperation and its importance for survival.* New York, NY: McGraw-Hill.

Jackson, T. (2004). *Management and change in Africa: Cross-cultural perspective.* New York, NY: Routledge.

James, R. (1998). Demystifying organization development: Practical experiences in African NGOs. *INTRAC.*

James, R. (2002a). *People and change: Exploring capacity building in Africa.* Oxford, England: INTRAC.

James, R. (2002b). What makes CSO coalitions effective? Lessons from Malawi. *INTRAC_Occasional Paper Series, 38,* 1–42.

Johnson, K. R., Head, T., & Sorensen, P. F. (1989). Proposed models for the reporting of cross-cultural OD interventions: A critique and proposed paradigm for OD evaluations. *Academy of Management Best Papers Proceedings, Academy of Management.*

Jones, M. (1988). Managerial thinking: An African perspective. *Journal of Management Studies, 25*(5), 481–505.

Jones, M., & Mann, P. (1983). Management development: An African perspective. In M. Jones & P. Mann (Eds.). *HRD: International perspectives on human resource development.* London, England: Kumarian.

Kerber, K. W., & Buono, A. F. (2009). Building change capacity: Client consultant collaboration and organizational change. In A. F. Buono & F. Poulfelt (Eds.), *Client consultant collaboration: Coping with complexity and change* (pp. 69–87). Charlotte, NC: Information Age.

Mangaliso, M. P. (2001). Building competitive advantage from Ubuntu: Management lessons from South Africa. *Academy of Management Executive, 15*(3), 23–33.

Sulamoyo, D. S. (2011). *A meta-analysis of organization development (OD) in Malawi and South Africa: The measurement of success rates.* Published dissertation. Benedictine University, Lisle, IL.

Vicars, W. M., & Hartke, D. D. (1984). Evaluating OD evaluations: A status report. *Group & Organization Studies, 9*(2), 177–188.

Woodman, R. W., & Sherwood, J. J. (1980). Effects of team development intervention: A field experiment. *Journal of Applied Behavioral Science, 16,* 211–227.

Woodman, R. W., & Wayne, S. J. (1985). An investigation of positive-findings bias in evaluation of organization development interventions. *Academy of Management Journal, 28,* 889–913.

6

The Future of OD in Southern Africa

Do not look where you fell, but where you slipped.
—African Proverb

OD faces many challenges in Africa. Since OD is fairly young in many parts of Africa, one of the challenges that practitioners have is effectively communicating and selling its value. There is a perception that it is a waste of resources. Practitioners need to focus on tying OD to organizational performance and profit margins. The fact that studies such as the one discussed in the previous chapter can demonstrate high success rates is impetus for OD's growth in Africa.

Another challenge that OD has is that more resources are going into project activities than into organizational learning in Africa. This has an impact on contextualization or indigenization. If fewer resources are allocated to learning, then less time is spent on ensuring that OD models and applications are conveyed effectively in different cultural settings.

As Africa continues to go through transitions, emerging transitional issues may need fields like OD to provide their successful facilitation. This concluding chapter explores these emerging transitional issues with the purpose of identifying some opportunities for OD.

Creating Opportunities for Change and OD in Southern Africa, pages 115–137

This chapter focuses on ideas and thoughts from the author that could be opportunities for OD in southern Africa. The sections of this chapter are presented as concepts and stories that help to define these opportunities for OD in southern Africa.

Large-System Changes and Rebuilding

Africa is currently agitating for large-system change. This agitation for change has occurred historically through pivotal periods in the continent's history. The movements for independence in the late 1950s and 1960s, movements for democratization in the early- to mid-1990s, and current winds of change promise to remove long-tenured authoritarian regimes and governments with autocratic tendencies. The year 2011 has certainly been etched in history as the year for revolutionary change. Revolutions in Tunisia, Egypt, Syria, and Libya have inspired the rest of the continent to place despot leaders on notice. In Malawi, massive demonstrations against the government of Bingu wa Mutharika took place in July 2011 due to the country's dissatisfaction with the current state of affairs and the ruler's growing autocratic stance.

Civil societies and NGOs played a critical role in engaging the public in the demonstrations and in negotiating with the government certain changes that need to occur. What role should OD play not only in facilitating political transitions but also in helping to rebuild once change has occurred? Transitions were part of the study discussed in the previous chapter. In South Africa, OD continues to play the critical role of facilitating the transition within organizations of the inclusion of Black South Africans. OD also continues to play the role of building effective teams between two groups of people that previously had conflict. For example, in Malawi, OD has played a critical role with organizations fighting the HIV/AIDS pandemic, and OD has helped build civil society organizations (CSOs). These CSOs represent a fourth branch of government that provides additional checks and balances in a political structure in which the three branches (executive, legislative, and judiciary) may not always effectively provide that balance. In countries going through transitions, OD can also help build effective systems, structures, and processes, and help develop leaders and foster organizational cultures that embrace the values of democracy, optimism, and humanism.

The Informal Economy

The informal economy is defined as the other sector that has activities involving the manufacture and trade of products, raw materials, and services without complying with regulations that apply to trade, commerce, and industry of a country. In Malawi, for instance, the 1990s saw a sharp increase in urban areas of vendors who traded goods and services in the informal sector. They set up their places of businesses in areas where formal businesses operated. They sold everything from clothes and food to bootleg DVDs, equipment, and services. Their presence in the formal areas of business was not well received because some of the vendors were involved in criminal activities and because the appearance of their business setup was an eyesore to some. The term "vendor" has negative connotations and in Malawi may be used pejoratively because of such informal setup. However, many Malawians who cannot afford to purchase their goods and services in the formal sector rely on the vendors for affordability of such items.

The past few decades have witnessed significant growth of the informal economic sector in Africa. Becker notes the following:

> Estimates show that the nonagricultural employment share of the informal workforce is 78% in Africa, 57% in Latin America and the Caribbean, and 45–85% in Asia. In all developing countries, self-employment comprises a greater share of informal employment than wage employment. Specifically, self-employment represents 70% of informal employment in Sub-Saharan Africa (if South Africa is excluded, the share is 81%), 62% in North Africa. (2004, p. 3)

The skills of those engaged in the informal sector have to be addressed, either for integrating them into the formal economy or for helping them to become more profitable in the informal sector.

> Training those who participate in the informal sector should go hand-in-hand with other instruments, such as fiscal policies, provision of credit, and extension of social protection and labor laws, to improve the performance of enterprises and the employability of workers. The aim should be to transform what is often marginal, survival activities into decent work fully integrated into mainstream economic life. (African Economic Outlook, 2008)

The field of OD has an opportunity to engage this sector with strategies and applications that facilitate performance improvement, knowledge exchange, development of processes and procedures, and the building of formal structures within that sector. Most African countries have accepted the presence of this informal sector. However, it is critical that participants in this sector are engaged with strategies for change that are mutually beneficial with the formal sector.

The Presence of China in Africa

Over the past decade, China has positioned itself as a critical player for aid and development in Africa. African countries with strained relationships with the West have been driven to the Chinese for partnerships in development and trade. Countries such as Malawi, which had relationships with the Taiwanese government for many years, have broken those relationships for new relationships with mainland China. As China's influence and control continue to grow in Africa, there arise issues that need to be addressed from an OD and management perspective. African countries that were former colonies have adopted systems of management from their former colonial masters. These systems have been imbued with their local and cultural approaches. What systems of management do the Chinese bring with their presence in Africa? How will their approach to management and change interface with what is in existence? Can African countries successfully develop their own indigenous systems while there are influences from the West and China because of aid and assistance?

The fact that OD is having a growing presence in China (Wang, 2011) is hope for its growing presence in Africa, particularly if the Chinese accept its importance in Africa as well. OD can play a critical role in facilitating cultural synergy between the Chinese and the Africans, particularly with the recognition of the importance of indigenization to OD.

Team Building in Southern Africa

The development and management of teams are areas of organization development that should be of interest to organizations and industries that hope to be competitive, relevant, and successful in a global economy. The approach to team development and the facilitation of effective teams can be influenced by the culture and history of an organization and the country in which it is based. It is important to understand the collectivist culture of Africa and its leadership models if teams are to be led effectively. The challenges for developing effective teams in some parts of southern Africa as a region in transition are based on overcoming past conflict and ensuring inclusivity of a society that is multicultural, multiethnic, multireligious, and sometimes multilingual.

Cultural Synergy Model

The cultural synergy model developed by Preston and Armstrong (1991) facilitates team building, particularly in places where cultural clashing is an impediment to development. Preston and Armstrong define this model as "a catalyst which empowers a new culture to use the best elements of individuals and their cultures. This creates an environment of openness and trust that induces permeability between individuals and the group. Awareness increases enabling creative problem solving to occur" (p. 66). This model has the following key elements: culture, synergy, systems, and creative problem solving.

In 1985, Preston and Armstrong applied this action research model to South Africa prior to the end of Apartheid to a group of business and community leaders who were Afrikaner and Black. The purpose of the exercise was to create opportunities for social change in South Africa from a team-based approach. The methodology of the synergy model included four steps. The first step involved the group's working separately to develop elements that would create cultural synergy for the group. This first step developed a set of norms for the group. Once they were developed, the second step involved the group's being brought together to agree on some common goals. This second step was critical in that it set the stage for how well the group would work together. During the third stage, the groups were mixed up so that people from the same culture were working with people from other cultures. They were given a major topic to solve and then expected to report back to the group as a whole. The enthusiasm that was felt during the reporting out phase of the process was a major factor toward team building (Preston & Armstrong, 1991, p. 78–79).

Tuckman's Model

Tuckman (1965) developed his model for understanding team development. This model can be used to contextualize other relationship developments both in organizations and in personal settings. It should be a foundation for linear progressive models because of its simplicity in explaining a very complex process. Tuckman's model has four stages of progressive development, which range from orientation of the group to performance. The four steps of his model are form, storm, norm, and perform. Tuckman's team development model has been combined with the cultural synergy model in Figure 6.1 to make it more applicable in some parts of southern Africa. This model can be used to understand the process of team development in the African context, particularly in a transitional setting. Bringing together groups that were involved in past conflict for the purposes of forming a team would be difficult without the "storming" stage occurring as the initiator of the group process. During this stage, conflict

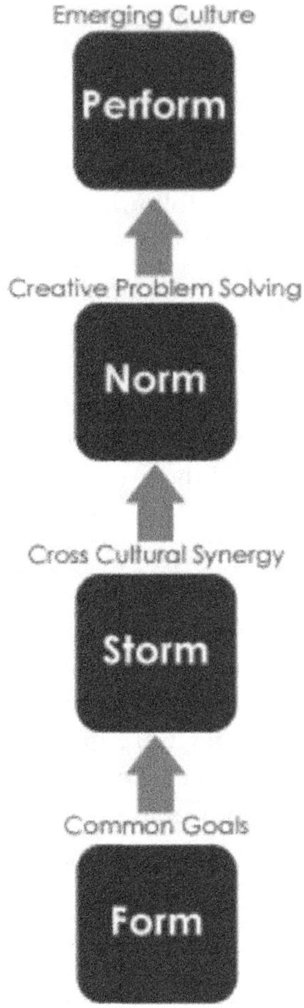

Figure 6.1 Team Development Model and the Cultural Synergy model (Adapted from Tuckman (1965) and Preston and Armstrong (1991)

resolution methodologies would be applied for purposes of overcoming past conflict and cultural clashing.

Once the "storming" stage has occurred, the team would go through "forming," wherein the cross-cultural synergy would occur. At this stage, the group would get to know each other and come together as a group (once the group formation is established, the group "norms") agreeing to how it would operate or function as a group. Effective performance would then occur after this stage in the process.

Applying Leadership Team Models in Southern Africa

How does Hackman's model of managing leadership teams and leading teams fit into the African setting? Hackman's (2002) model provides the enabling conditions for effectively leading teams: compelling direction, an enabling structure, a supportive context, and expert coaching. These enabling conditions are identified by Hackman as conditions necessary for effective teams. How do you ensure these conditions when you are dealing with past conflict or transition? How do you create conditions necessary for effective teams to overcome conflict? The cultural synergy model developed by Preston and Armstrong (1991), or models like it, should be utilized before efforts for effective teams are undertaken. The argument here is that the conditions identified by Hackman can be made available within an organizational context in Africa, but if conflict issues or cultural issues are not resolved beforehand, those efforts could be futile.

Given Africa's collectivist culture, leadership models, and transitional history, analyzing each one of the enabling conditions within that context would assess the Hackman (2002) model's applicability in Africa. What would be the appropriate enabling structure given past inequalities based on race and ethnicity? How do you define a real team in Africa? How do you provide compelling direction to a multicultural team? How do you ensure that leadership is not viewed as a means to dominate or subjugate? And finally, how do you ensure that capacity is built through coaching and interventions?

The second part of the discussion on teams involves leadership team models by Wageman, Nunes, Burruss, and Hackman (2008). The purpose of the study was to determine what makes senior teams great. The enabling conditions for effective teams are similar to those identified for general teams; however, for leadership teams, there is an emphasis on ensuring that the right people are in place. Wageman et al. (2008) identified four leadership team models: information-sharing teams, consultative teams, coordinating teams, and decision-making teams (pp. 36–39).

In exploring the effectiveness of leadership teams in Africa, the models for leadership teams identified by Wageman et al. (2008) are illustrated in Figure 6.2 as components of a developmental process for leadership teams in a transitional setting. Each one of the models could be a developmental stage for leadership teams, with the goal of effectiveness in decision making as the final stage of development. Wageman et al.'s leadership team models are illustrated in a proposed developmental model with values that, once attained, can move the team into the next phase of development.

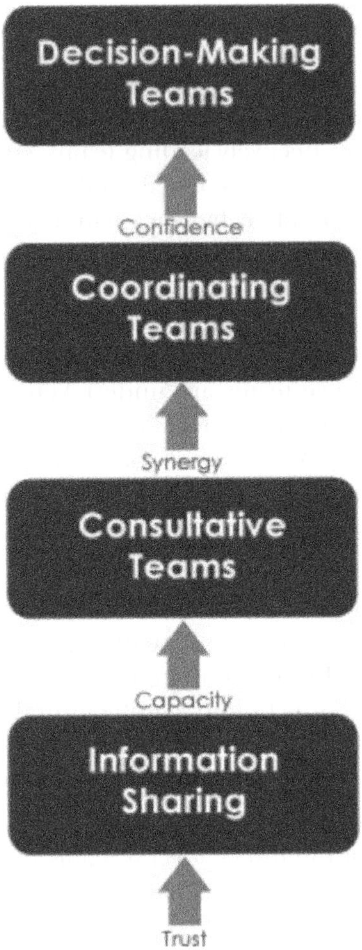

Figure 6.2 Transitional Leadership Team Development model. Leadership models adapted from Wageman et al. (2008).

Information-Sharing Teams (Trust)

To build a leadership team in a setting in which there has been cultural clashing and past conflict, information sharing is critical toward the formation of an effective team. According to Wageman et al. (2008), "Informational leadership teams exchange important information about various areas of the business and gather in one place external intelligence that may be useful to other parts of the organization" (p. 36). Information sharing cannot occur unless there is a building of trust among the team members involved. When Apartheid ended in South Africa, the organizational leadership structures dominated by White South Africans did not immediately become inclusive. Trust is still a major factor that is needed on both sides for inclusivity to occur. Inclusivity, in this case, is based on information sharing. In other places where there has been domination of one group over another, the first step for leadership team formation is trust, a critical first step toward an effective leadership team. Currently, in Zimbabwe, the government is a fledgling coalition made up of the ruling party and the main opposition party. Because there is no trust between the coalition members, progress toward a democratic resolution has stalled in Zimbabwe. According to Acemoglu, Egorov, and Sonin (2008),

> Because of the absence of strong, well-functioning institutions, binding agreements are not possible. This has two important implications: first, members of the ruling coalition cannot make binding offers on how resources will be distributed; second, and more importantly, members of a candidate ruling coalition cannot commit to not eliminating (sidelining) fellow members in the future. Consequently, there is always the danger that once a particular coalition has formed and has centralized power in its hands, a sub-coalition will try to remove some of the original members of the coalition in order to increase the share of resources allocated to itself. (p. 987)

Consultative Teams (Capacity)

Once the team has established trust and shared information, the next step involves capacity building for the leadership team members to be knowledgeable and develop expertise in their respective areas. Wageman et al. (2008) define consultative teams as teams that "actively debate key issues, giving members the chance to learn from one another" (p. 37). For consulting to occur among the team members, there has to be knowledge and expertise that result from capacity building. The challenge in some parts of Africa could be the existence of a capacity gap due to inequalities created from cultural domination and past conflict.

Coordinating Teams (Synergy)

The third step in this leadership team developmental process is the coordinating team. Wageman et al. (2008) define this type of team as one that "manages the operational interdependencies of the enterprise. Members of the coordinating teams are highly interdependent, have shared responsibilities, and must work together frequently and flexibly to accomplish their shared purpose" (p. 38). Coordination among these team members would occur if there was synergy. The word synergy is derived from the Greek word *synergos,* which means "working together." In business usage, *synergy* refers to the ability of two or more units or companies to generate greater value working together than they could by working apart (Goold & Campbell, 1998, p. 133). Goold and Campbell also identified six different forms or types of business synergy models: Shared Know-how, Coordinated Strategies, Shared Tangible Resources, Vertical Integration, Pooled Negotiating Power, and Combined Business Creation.

Decision-Making Teams (Confidence)

The fourth and final stage in the leadership team development process is the decision-making team. This stage is the highest stage for leadership teams in the developmental paradigm. Wageman et al. (2008) describe this type of team as responsible for making "the small number of critical decisions that are most consequential for the enterprise as a whole" (p. 38). Confidence would have to be one of the key attributes that would elevate a leadership team to be in a position of decision making. If the team possesses trust, capacity, and synergy, then confidence would enable the team to make decisions.

OD Consulting in Southern Africa

It could be argued that the role and art of consulting is something that has been around since biblical times. Priests, prophets, and other leaders of faith could perhaps represent spiritual consultants of God who have found their calling or were divinely chosen to advise and guide people to understand their God with the ultimate goal of salvation. These individuals, just like modern-day consultants, bring with them a high level of expertise and knowledge, which gives them the credibility to guide and facilitate people and organizations through change and development. In some societies like that of the Chewas of Malawi, elders are considered experts on cultural matters. These are matters pertaining to marriage customs, funeral rites, rites of passage, and the wisdom of bringing up children into responsible adults. In a sense, these elders are consultants of the Chewa society. They are the ones to whom people go for help and guidance. Organization development consulting at group, individual, or organizational levels should not be a foreign concept since it exists in cultural forms. Southern Africa's organizations need to understand that consultants bear great responsibility with the knowledge and expertise they possess to earn the trust of organizational leaders and staff to change the status quo of their organizations. Change is a process that is traumatic for people and organizations because it is a shift from what they know to something new and perhaps something that is uncomfortable. What role then should consultants play in facilitating change for organizations in southern Africa? What values does consulting possess?

The Role of Consulting

Consultants play different roles within organizations. This section will address their structural role and the personal role they play when dealing with organizations. Depending on its needs, an organization can seek the help of a consultant from outside the organization or can use an employee whose role would be to provide internal consulting. The difference between the two could be defined through a contract for an external consultant and an employment agreement for an internal consultant. However, how they apply their expertise to assist organizations through change should not differ that much.

Consultants can provide their technical assistance to an organization through training, advice, and guidance through a change process. As mentioned earlier, change can be a traumatic experience for organizations, and consultants sometimes play the role of comforting organizations through the change process. It is essential that trust is developed between a consultant and the client organization because the consultant gains access to critical information about the organization. Trust is essential to relationship-building in southern Africa. The trust has to be assured through a relationship such as the ones found in the medical and legal fields of attorney-client or doctor-patient privileged relationships. It should be the goal of the consultant to create independence for the organization through their services in the long term. Consulting should be a reciprocal learning opportunity for the client and consultant. No two organizations are going to be exactly alike. Consequently, each consulting opportunity should be a learning opportunity to increase the knowledge and expertise about organizations.

The Value of OD Consulting

Organizations in southern Africa need to find value in OD consulting. Consultants bring a lot of value to organizations. Many organizations do not have the internal capacity or expertise to engage in change projects. In some cases, organizations do not have the resources to invest in long-term change initiatives. An option they may take involves bringing in external consultants to conduct specific interventions. Consultants possess an external lens into the organization that may help to affirm or to challenge the direction that organization may have chosen for its change initiative. Consultants' experience and knowledge, combined with critical thinking skills, are what organizations need when dealing with the chaos of change. The ultimate value that an organization should obtain through a relationship with a consultant is knowledge transfer. An organization should develop its own internal expertise with the change initiative through the consultant. In other words, the consultant offers a vessel or container of knowledge for the organization. This is critical if African organizations are to foster self-sufficiency and become the creators of new organizational knowledge that benefits other organizations.

Crisis Assessment and Management

Any environment, particularly those of organizations in Africa, can be dynamic, with changes sometimes leading to crisis. It is critical for African organizations to master crisis management for their survivability. According to Preble (1997), "Crisis management is defined as a systematic process by which an organization attempts to predict or identify potential crises that an organization many encounter, take precautions to prevent the crises or minimize the effects of the crises" (p. 777). A crisis management model has an OD approach because it utilizes the whole-systems approach, which is based on action research. Teams are utilized to plan the process. A crisis management model calls for an internal and external assessment, which serves as the diagnosis. Change strategies are then developed with evaluation and monitoring of the whole framework, and its findings are conducted on an ongoing basis. Information learned in the assessment is developed into strategies that are regularly evaluated. All areas of an organization—from human resources to fiscal operations, facilities, funding, and resources—are considered for the assessment, and strategies are developed to prevent crises or to mitigate them. This process should be facilitated by an OD consultant to ensure that the humanistic, democratic, and optimistic values of OD are prevalent in both the responses and the management of crises.

Sensemaking and Diagnosis for Future Interventions

Crises interventions and the management of crises should perhaps be the roles of OD consultants because of the change dimensions that occur in a crisis or the response to unplanned change by organizations. An important process associated with change and crisis events is *sensemaking*—understanding what happened and why it happened. OD consultants could use techniques such as large-group methods or strength-based approaches such as appreciative inquiry to diagnose what went wrong and why so that they can design future interventions for more planned changes. If organizations can learn from the experience of an unplanned event or crisis, then perhaps changes planned from that experience could be sustainable. If OD consultants go into an organization only after a crisis event, they could find themselves at a disadvantage, particularly if the organization has not completed its sensemaking process. Their interventions may not be sustainable. Maitlis and Sonenshein (2010) argue for the convergence of crises management and change through sensemaking because of their revolutionary and evolutionary similarities (p. 552).

OD consultants are needed now more than ever in southern Africa because of the fast paced and dynamic environments that organizations are operating in today. Organizations are more likely to experience unplanned change/events or crises in an environment that can perhaps be characterized as being volatile. The role of OD consultants cannot be limited to facilitated planned changes. They should be involved in crises interventions, management, and sensemaking as an approach to laying the groundwork for planned change in organizations in southern Africa.

OD and the Political Framework in Southern Africa

At the center of Africa's problems are the issues of governance mired in political structures that are legacies of the past colonial regimes. Former British colonies such as Malawi, Zambia, and Zimbabwe have parliamentary systems that, for the most part, mirror the British system. Business in Parliament is conducted in the English language. The speaker and clerks of Parliament wear robes with white wigs, and male members of Parliament wear Western-styled suits. It is interesting that after many years of independence, the legacies of the colonial systems are still entrenched in the political systems of southern Africa. Could some of the governance problems experienced by countries in southern Africa be attributable to an inherited Western-developed structure that does not quite fit within an indigenous setting? Could the mimicry of Western political culture by African governments be at the center of failed states? How would indigenously grown systems and structures contribute to the stability of southern African governments? Could African-grown political systems and structures become accepted as legitimate by the West? How could they interact and become integrated with the rest of the world?

These are indeed big questions that could take many years to address. However, issues of governance embedded in these political systems and structures have an impact on southern Africa's ability to develop. There may be opportunities for OD to play a role in offering to governance alternative approaches that are homegrown. OD could aid in facilitating the indigenization of these political systems that are still very Western influenced and grown. For instance, new dispensations of government that have emerged in the postautocratic regime era have emphasized participatory democracy. However, the participation of the citizenry in the political process is an exercise that occurs only during elections. This is not a guarantee; elections in southern Africa are marred with alleged vote rigging, intimidation, and political violence. The voice of the citizenry is not always represented in policy making. Nongovernmental organizations (NGOs) and civil society organizations (CSOs) are playing a role in ensuring that the voice of the citizenry is heard in the policy-making arena. However, there could be more direct participation by the citizenry in the process.

Most political parties in countries like Malawi develop manifestos to represent their policy positions in various areas that government has an impact. These are areas not limited to education, health care, agriculture, trade, governance, and fighting corruption. The manifesto represents a blueprint that a political party adopts to represent its strategies once the party is successful in winning an election and forming the next government. This is no different from policy positions that candidates take when running for office in the United States. One aspect that is common between manifestos in southern Africa and policy positions developed by candidates running for office in the United States is the fact that the essential development of these positions does not involve the engagement of the voters. These are positions that are developed with the help of intellectuals and experts in the various areas addressed by manifesto. The political parties and candidates then campaign on these positions to convince the electorate why their positions would be better for the country's development and growth.

The Framework

This section of the chapter presents an opportunity for developing political party manifestos using OD as the facilitator. The framework presented here is basically a proposed model that could be adopted by the political parties of southern Africa. The African electorate must require accountable and transparent governments as the new basis for national development. African countries must strive to cultivate peaceful and stable atmospheres to foster development and to establish modern democratic governments. These efforts would increase their economic competitiveness to meet the challenges of globalization and regional economies, to create dynamic and plural civil societies, and to foster living environments that enable sustainable development.

In many southern African cultures, large group meetings are convened by community leaders and chiefs to discuss issues affecting the community as a whole. Some of the local terms for these meetings are *pungwe* (Zimbabwe), *indaba* (South Africa and cultures of Zulu descent), and *pabwalo* (Malawi). In some cultures, these meetings involve only certain persons with rank in the community, but in most cultures the community as whole is encouraged to participate. The proposed political framework for southern Africa would be modeled after these large group meetings as a facilitated dialogue between political parties and the electorate. These dialogues would be designed to engage the electorate from all walks of life of a particular country, meaning that strategies for progress and development would not be left only to the elite to develop. The common person would have a say not only in the voting booth but even before elections take place. The facilitated dialogues would have the following fundamental values:

- Bottom-up public participation process in politics
- Responsibility and accountability
- Proactive and comprehensive risk management
- Political decisions based on the people's practical daily living experience
- Independent evaluation of government performance in all sectors

Political parties in southern Africa should reinvent themselves by shifting their paradigm from the usual and predictable behavior of political entities by making their process of developing manifestos a process for the people and by the people. Many political parties and governments think of engaging the electorate only during elections but not in decision making. The electorate needs to be engaged and empowered to be part of the decision-making process before, during, and after elections. The process for developing the manifestos needs to be transparent, with a grassroots approach.

The political manifestos need to be developed as a result of strategic planning processes that engage the electorate in facilitated dialogues from all sectors of a country's economy. The development of the manifestos should not be limited only to the elites and recognized intellects but should be a facilitated process that emanates from the grassroots by focusing on an identified cross section of a country's community. Everyone from peasants to doctors, students to teachers, and merchants to economists should be engaged in what they hope for in terms of policies in the various areas that impact their livelihood as citizens. What agricultural policies do peasants want that improve their livelihood in the rural area? What do students want out of educational policy to secure their future after they are finished with schooling? This framework should allow the local farmer to have a say in agricultural policies. Doctors, nurses, and pharmacists should have a say in health policies. Educators should have a say in education policies. Citizenry from all walks of life should have a say in policies that impact their livelihood. The party leadership together with policy experts should then frame recommendations from this process into policy initiatives that become part of the manifesto.

Dialogue with the electorate is proposed to be one of the best ways to capture the nation's position, reaction, and response to current economic and social conditions. By organizing a group of citizens, leaders, and stakeholders, the political parties will learn and understand the conditions within the country that create and prolong poverty and obstruct development. This forum could offer an opportunity to raise awareness, strategize with, and organize key players into resolving issues and implementing effective, viable strategies to move the citizenry of southern Africa's countries out of poverty toward self-sufficiency.

Manifesto Development Process

The manifesto development process is proposed to be cyclical. It includes seven components: public dialogue, policy synthesis, manifesto development, release of manifesto, opposition policies, policy implementation, and evaluation of government policies. Figure 6.3 illustrates a model of the framework for the manifesto development process.

Step 1: Public Dialogue

The process should begin with a public dialogue, which would essentially be the convening of people from all walks of life to discuss issues affecting their community or country as a whole. This discussion would be done much like many large group meetings that are part of most cultures in southern Africa.

The following are purposes for convening a public dialogue to develop a manifesto:

1. To take action at the local district, regional, and national levels to address the most pressing problems affecting individuals, families, businesses, farmers, and communities.

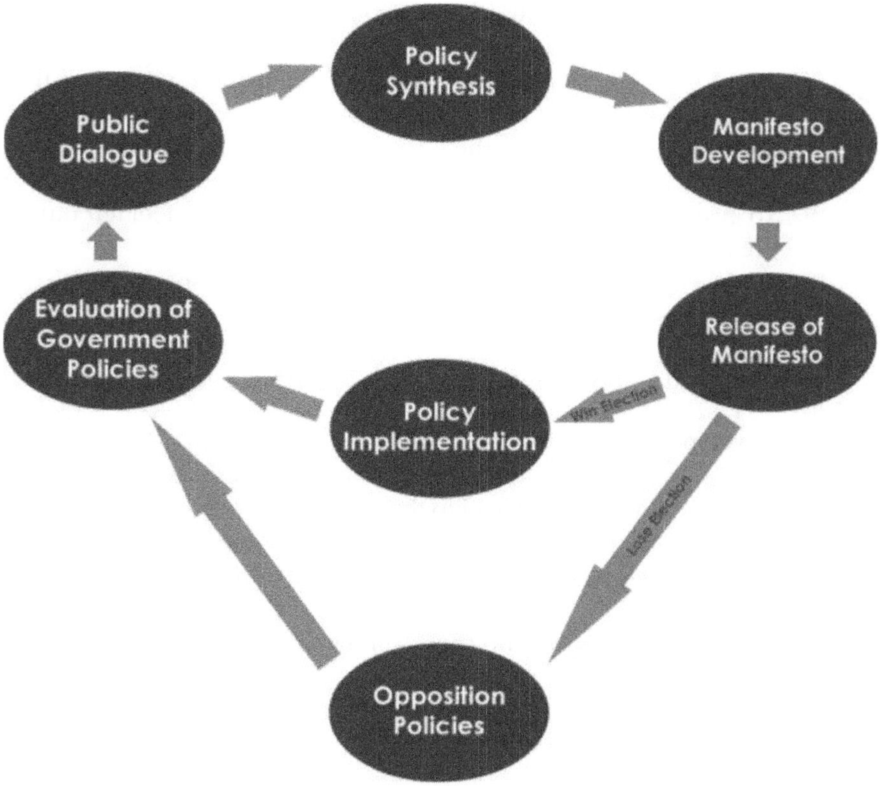

Figure 6.3 Political party manifesto development process.

2. To restore a sense of hope that, working together, common goals can be achieved.
3. To direct resources to different parts of the country to get the results people want for all individuals and families.
4. To create an opportunity for people from different parts of the country to come together in dialogue about the issues affecting their country.
5. To provide an opportunity for local people who ordinarily are not involved in policy-making decisions to become a central part of the dialogue that will lead to new solutions to address the problems that face their country.
6. To focus and strengthen commitments from individuals, organizations, businesses, and governments to devote necessary resources to achieve new outcomes for the citizenry.

7. To pool community knowledge about the problems facing a cross section of communities and solutions for resolving them.
8. To inform and educate public officials, the private sector, and the public at-large about the current problems faced by a nation and the strategies to combat them through a contract with the political parties.
9. To give a voice to persons from all walks of life who feel left out of the decision-making process.
10. To develop and support community leadership, especially with a cross section of the citizenry.

The roles and responsibilities of political parties are as follows:

1. Develop resources for the dialogues
2. Develop resources for the policy development sessions following the dialogues, which would lead to the development of the manifesto.
3. Strategically select where the dialogues will take place.
4. Select trusted party functionaries who can coordinate local dialogues.
5. Select policy experts who can formulate policy positions from results of the dialogues.

The roles and responsibilities of the local dialogue coordinator are as follows:

1. Understand the value, purposes, and process of the local dialogue.
2. Develop a local plan for the dialogue.
3. Identify and/or obtain the resources needed for dialogue from the party.
4. Identify who will be involved and then develop and implement ways to involve them.
5. Identify and obtain use of sites to be used for the dialogue.
6. Identify and train facilitators.
7. Identify and obtain all necessary supplies and materials.
8. Arrange necessary support for participants, for example, transportation and refreshments.
9. Ensure that the sites and facilitators are operating effectively.
10. Ensure that materials, supplies, and necessary support for participants are available.
11. Address problems that may emerge.
12. Collect data from the dialogue process.

Step 2: Policy Synthesis

Once the public dialogues have taken place, the data gathered from that process needs to be synthesized by policy experts into policy positions. For instance, if farmers participating in the public dialogues identified the fact that it was difficult for them to grow healthy crops because of the high cost of fertilizer, then the policy experts could synthesize that fact into a policy on fertilizer subsidies that would assist the farmers. If parents participating in the dialogues identified that it was costly for them to send their children to school, then the policy experts could synthesize this fact into a policy on free primary or secondary school education. This approach ensures that policy positions outlined in the manifesto are a direct response to the needs of the people.

Step 3: Release of the Manifesto

Once the policy positions have been developed, the manifesto would be released to the public. The release of the manifesto would essentially become the platform on which a political party would conduct its campaign. Most southern African political parties in countries such as Malawi are not necessarily ideologically based. Policies outlined in their manifestos essentially represent their approach on governance.

Step 4: Policy Implementation

If a political party is successful in its campaign for parliamentary or presidential elections, then its members would have an opportunity to implement the policies outlined in the manifesto. This approach would again ensure that the government or members of parliament are responsive to the electorate.

Step 5: Opposition Policies

If a political party is not successful in the election, then it can use its policies outlined in the manifesto to effectively debate the government. In some countries, a shadow administration to the government is established for purposes of offering an effective opposition. Opposition policies in this model should also be used to gain compromises when implementing government policies.

Step 6: Evaluation of Government Policies

A time frame must be built into the evaluation of government's policies after implementation. This does not always have to be done during an election period. Both the public and the opposition would need to evaluate these policies on their merits as well as on the merits of alternative policies.

Appreciative Inquiry and Transitions in Southern Africa

Yaeger, Head, and Sorensen (2006) identified appreciative inquiry (AI) as one of OD's interventions that has universal applicability in both economic and cultural contexts (p. 53). Why and how is AI universally applicable? How much of its applicability is adaptability? According to Yaeger and Bengtsson (2001), the process of implementing AI can vary (p. 446), probably due to the existence of organizational culture and other factors. However, a common theme is identified that transcends all subcultural traits—the recollection of peak experiences. Yaeger and Bengtsson (2001) defined peak experiences as moments when individuals reflect on the best in themselves and their organizations through positive storytelling. Everyone should have a peak experience within the context of an organization. The peak experiences do not have to be similar. What is similar here is that everyone has experienced peak moments within the context of organizations.

Appreciative inquiry certainly has been ranked as one of the few interventions of OD that has universal applicability, because of its commonality in peak experiences across cultures. AI may need to be considered by global OD change agents as not only the cultural and economic integrator but also as the facilitator of other interventions to be successfully adaptable in otherwise inhospitable conditions.

Could AI be applicable in negotiations for peace and political compromise? Appreciative inquiry could be applied to rebuild societies that are emerging out of conflict or to facilitate opposing groups to work toward a common goal. The process could focus on what made these groups great and the strengths they each possess to move their societies forward. There can be little doubt that different groups or political parties in southern Africa have a great love for their countries. The differences arise based on direction, ethnicity, politics, and control. If AI were utilized to get differing groups to focus on what they can agree on, perhaps rebuilding could begin from that standpoint.

Inspiring Hope

A few years ago, I visited an AIDS orphanage in Malawi. This orphanage is located in a remote rural part of the country close to the border between Zambia and Malawi. My family is closely associated with this orphanage: my mother serves on its board as a trustee and my brother and I have raised funds for the orphanage here in the United States. This orphanage houses infants, toddlers, and young adults attending high school. Most of these children have lost their parents to AIDS. Even though most of these orphans have family that could take care of them in the absence of their parents, that type of family commitment has been more difficult to fulfill with the abject poverty prevalent throughout Malawi and the overwhelming increase in orphans. Most families can barely feed themselves let alone additional children.

When we arrived there, the older children came outside to greet my family with several traditional dances as a celebration of our visit. I had the opportunity to interview about 15 of these children on camera. When I first met this group of orphans, my initial reaction was pity that their futures were bleak based on the circumstances and the predicament in which they found themselves. I basically had condemned their futures based on my own bias brought about by my observation of their situation and environment. However, I decided to find out more about them through an appreciative interview. I had decided not to ask how they ended up in an orphanage for fear of evoking emotions of their loss. I personally did not know how I would have handled such a personal outburst of emotion because the environment was quite overwhelming.

What transpired as a result of the responses from these orphans was a transformation of my outlook on their situation from a negative one to one that was full of hope, dreams, and great expectations. These children had dreams and aspirations of becoming doctors, teachers, lawyers, nurses, and for some, politicians. What right did I have to condemn not only their futures but their ability to dream? None of the children I interviewed felt that their future was bleak and condemned because of the difficult circumstances in which they found themselves. None of them felt pity for themselves or for each other. They had bright smiles and a positive general outlook on life. Each one of these 15 children taught me a valuable lesson: it is possible to dream in spite of your circumstances. They also taught me that we have the responsibility of ensuring that these children's dreams, and those of all children, should be realized with our help and encouragement, because the future of our community and the world rests with our children. Finally, they taught me that they each had strengths that, if effectively connected, could result in positive outcomes for their lives so that their orphaned predicament becomes irrelevant as a determinant of their future.

OD, Forgiveness, and Reconciliation in a Postconflict Era

Many remarkable stories in other parts of the continent of Africa inspire hope in places where there was conflict but now there is peace and development. The amazing attributes that people of Africa have for forgiveness and reconciliation must be considered as values of OD in postconflict work.

How do Malawians who suffered under the dictatorship of Dr. Banda forgive their tormentors and work side by side with them in the interest of the nation? How does Morgan Tsvangirai, the Prime Minister of Zimbabwe, who was tortured and imprisoned several times by his political nemesis, President Robert Mugabe, put those differences aside to work with him in the interest of nation building and recovery? How do Black South Africans who lost family members and suffered for many years during Apartheid avoid retribution for nation building?

In spite of the arguments made by Blunt (1995) and Jones and Mann (1983) that Africa is inhospitable to OD, attributes of forgiveness and reconciliation offer greater opportunities for OD to facilitate the rebuilding in southern Africa. If people can put their differences aside to focus on common interests, greater possibilities can be realized. OD needs to be positioned to offer hope where there is despair, courage where there is fear, and a light toward a brighter future where there is darkness and misery. Many countries have had major divisions, but those divisions have not escalated to civil conflict. OD needs to focus the attention on the strength of forgiveness and reconciliation as a means to effectively transition from conflict and past injustices.

Summary

This final chapter offers thoughts and ideas for the future of OD in southern Africa. The discussions in this chapter were not necessarily research based, but they were observations by the author and an exploration of ideas and concepts that could be further explored by OD experts in a southern African environment. The chapter thus addressed emerging national and transnational issues, applicability of specific OD interventions, models to be considered by the political framework, and the inspiration for hope based on the human resolve. There is indeed much room for OD's growth and utilization in southern Africa. Some of that growth is dependent upon the acceptance of indigenously developed management ideas by the mainstream of management.

References

Acemoglu, D., Egorov, G., Sonin, K. (2008). Coalition formation in non-democracies. *Review of Economic Studies, 75*(4), 987–1009.

African Economic Outlook. (2008). *Adressing the skill needs of the informal sector.* Retrieved from http://www.africaneconomicoutlook.org/en/in-depth/developing-technical-and-vocational-skills-in-africa-2008/lessons-learned-from-technical-and-vocational-skills-development-reforms/adressing-the-skill-needs-of-the-informal-sector/

Becker, K. F. (2004). *Fact finding study: The informal economy.* Stockholm, Sweden: Swedish International Development Cooperation Agency.

Blunt, P. (1995). The cultural limits of process consulting in development assistance. In R. Reineke and R. Sulzer (Eds). *Management consultancy in developing countries.* Berlin: Gabler.

Goold, M., & Campbell, A. (1998). Desperately seeking synergy. *Harvard Business Review, 76*(5), 131–143.

Hackman, J. R. (2002). *Leading teams: Setting the stage for great performances.* Boston, MA: Harvard Business School Press.

Jones, M., & Mann, P. 1983. Management development: An African perspective. In M. Jones, & P. Mann (Eds.). *HRD: International perspectives on human resource development.* London: Kumarian.

Maitlis, S., & Sonenshein, S. (2010). Sensemaking in crisis and change: Inspiration and insights from Weick (1988). *Journal of Management Studies, 47*(3), 551–580.

Preble, J. F. (1997). Integrating the crisis management perspective into the strategic management process. *Journal of Management Studies, 34*(5), 769–791.

Preston, J. C., & Armstrong, T. R. (1991). Team building in South Africa: Cross cultural synergy in action. *Public Administration Quarterly, 15*(1), 65–82.

Tuckman, B. W. (1965). Developmental sequence in small groups. *Psychological Bulletin, 63*(6), 384–399.

Wageman, R., Nunes, D. A., Burruss, J. A., & Hackman, J. R. (2008). *Senior leadership teams: What it takes to make them great.* Boston, MA: Harvard Business School Press.

Wang, X. (2011). *A descriptive study of organization development's relevant work reported in China between 1978 and 2010.* Published dissertation. Benedictine University, Lisle, IL.

Yaeger, T., & Bengtsson, U. (2001). Appreciative inquiry: Current perspectives from global consultants. In P. F. Sorensen, T. C. Head, T. Yaeger, & D. Cooperrider (Eds.), *Global and international organization development* (pp. 443–451). Champaign, IL: Stipes.

Yaeger, T. F., Head, T. C., & Sorensen, P. F. (2006). *Global organization development: Managing unprecedented change.* Greenwich, CT: Information Age.

APPENDIX

Literature Review on Organization Development Studies from Malawi and South Africa

Creating Opportunities for Change and OD in Southern Africa, pages 139–178

TABLE A.1 Literature Review on OD Studies From Malawi and South Africa

Authors	Title	Country	Purpose	Journal/ Publication
Koornhof, C. (2001)	Developing a framework for flexibility within organizations	South Africa	To define the construct of flexibility in organizations	*South African Journal of Business Management, 32*(4)
Horwitz, F. M., Anderssen, K. et al. (2002)	Due diligence neglected: Managing human resources and organizational culture in mergers and acquisitions	South Africa	To identify attributes of organizational culture and human resource practices required for successful transitions in mergers and acquisitions	*South African Journal of Business Management, 33*(1)
Terblanche, N. S. & Boshoff, C. (2006)	A generic instrument to measure customer satisfaction with the controllable elements of the in-store shopping experience	South Africa	To develop a generic instrument that could be used to measure customer satisfaction with the controllable elements of the in-store shopping experience	*South African Journal of Business Management, 37*(3)
Krosigk, B. V. (2007)	A holistic exploration of leadership development	South Africa	To present a holistic exploration of leadership development	*South African Journal of Business Management, 38*(2)
Co, M. J. (2003)	A sociocultural explanation of Black entrepreneurship in South Africa	South Africa	To explain why entrepreneurship levels among indigenous Africans are low by specifically using the sociocultural approach	*South African Journal of Business Management, 34*(4)
Morrison, J. M., Brown, C. J. et al. (2006)	A supportive organizational culture for project management in matrix organizations: A theoretical perspective	South Africa	Defining the supportive culture for project management in organizations	*South African Journal of Business Management, 37*(4)
Kriek, H. S. (2007)	A survey of the prevalence and nature of team-building interventions in South African organizations	South Africa	Exploration of the prevalence of team-building interventions in South African organizations	*South African Journal of Business Management, 38*(4)

(continued)

Authors	Title	Country	Purpose	Journal/ Publication
Durbach, I. N., & Parker, H. (2009)	An analysis of corporate board networks in South Africa	South Africa	Analysis of networks created by directors sitting on corporate boards in South Africa	*South African Business Journal, 40*(2)
Terblanche, N. S. (2006)	An application of the American customer satisfaction index (ACSI) in the South African motor vehicle industry	South Africa	Assessing the reliability of the American customer satisfaction index in South Africa	*South African Business Journal, 37*(4)
Van der Merwe, S. P. (2009)	An investigation of the determinants of estate and retirement planning in intergenerational family businesses	South Africa	To explore the determinants of estate and retirement planning	*South African Business Journal, 40*(3)
Grobler, P., Kirsten, A. M. et al. (2005)	Building capacity for their members: What employers' organizations in South Africa need to know	South Africa	To determine the use, efficiency, and effectiveness of employer organizations	*South African Business Journal, 36*(2)
De Klerk, S., & Kroon, J. (2008)	Business networking relationships for business success	South Africa	To explore the context of business relationships in the networking practices of South African businesses	*South African Business Journal, 39*(2)
Bruwer, B. W. S., & Hamman, W. D. (2006)	Company failure in South Africa: Classification and prediction by means of recursive partitioning	South Africa	The development of models for the classification and prediction of failed and nonfailed industrial companies in South Africa	*South African Business Journal, 37*(4)
De Villiers, P., & Kooy, G. (2004)	Contribution of worker participation to increase the efficiency of firms	South Africa	Worker participation as means to alleviate to inefficiencies in a firm	*South African Business Journal, 35*(3)
Hart, M. L. (2006)	Customer relationship management: Are software applications aligned with business objectives?	South Africa	Examination of the balance between strategy formulation, IT, and organizational alignment when adopting and implementing customer relationship management	*South African Business Journal, 37*(2)

(continued)

Authors	Title	Country	Purpose	Journal/ Publication
Van der Merwe, S. P. (2009)	Determinants of family employee work performance and compensation in family businesses.	South Africa	To empirically explore some of the determinants of family employee work performance and compensation in small- and medium-sized family businesses	*South African Business Journal, 40*(1)
Modares, A., & Sepehri, M. (2009)	Development of an integrated system for distribution planning in supply chain	South Africa	To introduce and describe a distribution planning system based on an innovative vehicle routing and scheduling problem classification scheme	*South African Business Journal, 40*(4)
Arnolds, C. A., & Boshoff, C. (2000)	Does higher remuneration equal higher job performance?: An empirical assessment of the need-progression proposition in selected need theories	South Africa	Theories of motivation have been the foundation of many interventions to increase employee job performance. A more advanced technique—structural equation analysis—which identifies what variable causes a certain outcome is used to measure the influence of various need satisfactions on performance intentions.	*South African Business Journal, 31*(2)
Mazibuko, N. E., & Boshoff, C. (2003)	Employee perceptions of share ownership schemes: An empirical study	South Africa	To investigate some of the problems associated with the introduction and successful management of Employee Share Ownership Schemes (ESOPs)	*South African Business Journal, 34*(2)
Lee, G. J., Venter, R. et al. (2004)	Enterprise-based HIV/AIDS strategies: Integration through organizational architecture	South Africa	To review varied literature on organizational architectures and then show how various HIV/AIDS policies and practices might fit into such an architecture	*South African Business Journal, 35*(3)
Van der Walt, R. (2008)	Have workplace forums contributed to worker participation? Some management perceptions	South Africa	To determine whether or not workplace forums have contributed to worker participation	*South African Business Journal, 39*(2)

(continued)

Authors	Title	Country	Purpose	Journal/ Publication
Cachia, A., & Kruger, C. J. (2007)	Guidelines for identifying risk vulnerabilities associated with ICT sourcing	South Africa	To develop guidelines for identifying risk vulnerabilities associated with ICT sourcing	*South African Business Journal, 38*(4)
Alexander, N. S., Bick, G. et al. (2009)	Impact of branding and product augmentation on decision making in the B2B market	South Africa	To investigate the impact of the brand and product augmentation on the buyers of industrial tires	*South African Business Journal, 40*(1)
Brown, C. J., & Botha, M. C. (2005)	Lessons learnt on implementing project management in a functionally only structured South African municipality	South Africa	To report on the most important lessons learned from the implementation of project management in a South African district municipality [and an] African district municipality	*South African Business Journal, 36*(4)
Rothmann, S. & Joubert, J. H. M. (2007)	Job demands, job resources, burnout and work engagement of managers at a platinum mine in the North West Province	South Africa	To investigate the relationships between job demands, job resources, burnout, and engagement of management staff at platinum mine in the North West Province	*South African Business Journal, 38*(3)
Buitendach, J. H., & De Witte, H. (2005)	Job insecurity, extrinsic and intrinsic job satisfaction and effective organizational commitment of maintenance workers in a parastatal	South Africa	To assess the relationship between job insecurity, job satisfaction, and affective organizational commitment of maintenance workers ($N = 178$) in a parastatal in Gauteng	*South African Business Journal, 36*(2)
Rothmann, S., Steyn, L. J. et al. (2005)	Job stress, sense of coherence and work wellness in an electricity supply organization	South Africa	To test a causal model of work wellness for engineers, technicians, and electricians in an electricity supply organization	*South African Business Journal, 36*(1)
Pretorius, C. J., & Steyn, H. (2005)	Knowledge management in project environments	South Africa	To review the literature on knowledge management, both in organizations in general and in project environments specifically	*South African Business Journal, 36*(3)

(continued)

Authors	Title	Country	Purpose	Journal/ Publication
Garg, A. K., Joubert, R. J. O. et al. (2005)	Information systems environmental alignment and business performance: A case study	South Africa	To explore the environmental alignment of information systems and business performance	*South African Business Journal, 36*(4)
Msweli-Mbanga, P., & Potwana, N. (2006)	Modeling participation, resistance to change, and organizational citizenship behavior: A South African case	South Africa	To establish the extent to which employees from state owned enterprises are provided with information and opportunities to participate in change efforts in their organizations and secondly, to verify the relationship between access to participation, willingness to participation, resistance to change, and organizational citizenship behavior by testing a model that links these four constructs together.	*South African Business Journal, 37*(1)
Boyd, G., & Sutherland, M. (2006)	Obtaining employee commitment to living the brand of the organization	South Africa	To determine the key success factors in obtaining employee commitment to living the brand of the organization by reviewing literature on the topic and using the scientific case study method of Yin (1984) to gather empirical data	*South African Business Journal, 37*(1)
Coetzer, W. J., & Rothmann, S. (2006)	Occupational stress of employees in an insurance company	South Africa	To assess the internal consistency of the ASSET, to identify occupational stressors for employees in an insurance company, and to assess the relationships between occupational stress, ill health, and organizational commitment	*South African Journal of Business Management, 37*(3)
Thomas, A., & Lindsay, D. (2003)	Organizational culture at a South African food service company	South Africa	To examine whether congruence exists between the organizational culture perceived to be evident at Compass, South Africa, and the strategic objectives of the company	*South African Business Journal, 34*(4)

(continued)

Authors	Title	Country	Purpose	Journal/ Publication
Smith, E. E., & Kruger, J. (2005)	Perception of graduates regarding workplace expectations: An exploratory study	South Africa	To outline the results of a study that investigates the perceptions of graduates regarding workplace expectations	*South African Business Journal, 36*(1)
Bick, G., Abratt, R. et al. (2008)	Perceptions of the corporate identity management process in South Africa	South Africa	To report on a qualitative study of how the corporate identity management process is perceived and managed by senior executives in large South African companies	*South African Business Journal, 39*(3)
Vermeulen, L. P., & Coetzee, M. (2006)	Perceptions of the dimensions of the fairness of affirmative action: A pilot study	South Africa	To identify the dimensions of affirmative action (AA) fairness in order to develop a valid and reliable questionnaire to assess employees' perceptions of the fairness of AA decisions and practices, and to explore the relationship between employees' biographical characteristics and their perceptions of the dimensions of AA fairness	*South African Business Journal, 37*(2)
Vogel, A. J., van Vuuren, J. J. et al. (2008)	Preparation, support and training requirements of South African expatriates	South Africa	To determine how South African global organizations should prepare, support, and train their expatriates for international assignments	*South African Business Journal, 39*(3)
Morrison, J., & Brown, C. (2004)	Project management effectiveness as a construct: A conceptual study	South Africa	To explore project management effectiveness	*South African Business Journal, 35*(4)
Boshoff, C., & Staude, G. (2003)	Satisfaction with service recovery: Its measurement and its outcomes	South Africa	To assess the validity and reliability of an instrument purported to measure satisfaction with service recovery (RECOVSAT) and to determine which dimensions of service recovery satisfaction are the most important predictors of overall satisfaction and loyalty	*South African Business Journal, 34*(3)

(continued)

Authors	Title	Country	Purpose	Journal/ Publication
Mansfield, G. M., & Fourie, L. C. H. (2004)	Strategy and business models—strange bedfellows? A case for convergence and its evolution into strategic architecture	South Africa	To explore sustainable competitive advantage through strategy	*South African Business Journal, 35*(1)
Lotz, T., & Donald, F. (2006)	Stress communication across job levels after an acquisition	South Africa	To investigate the relationship between employee satisfaction with the organizational communication that occurred during an acquisition and their experiences of stress	*South African Business Journal, 37*(1)
Fayazbakhsh, K., Sepehri, M. et al. (2009)	Supply chain coordination with flow networks	South Africa	To explore supply chain coordination with flow networks	*South African Business Journal, 40*(2)
Birt, M., Wallis, T. et al. (2004)	Talent retention in changing workplace: An investigation of variables considered important to South African talent	South Africa	To explore variables considered important to South African talent for talent retention	*South African Business Journal, 35*(2)
Esterhuyse, W. P. (2003)	The challenge of transformation: Breaking the barriers	South Africa	To discuss and perform a conceptual analysis of transformation	*South African Business Journal, 34*(3)
Buys, M. A., Olckers, C. et al. (2007)	The construct validity of the revised job diagnostic survey	South Africa	To examine how the Job Characteristics Model, the accompanying Job Diagnostic Survey (JDS), and the proposed steps for improving motivation, satisfaction, and performance have been functionally utilized in South Africa as a revised job redesign practice to address some critical human resources problems currently facing managers and human resources practitioners; and to determine the construct validity of the Revised Job Diagnostic Survey(JDS) in the South African context	*South African Business Journal, 38*(2)

(continued)

Authors	Title	Country	Purpose	Journal/ Publication
Fontannaz, S., & Oosthuizen, H. (2007)	The development of a conceptual framework to guide sustainable organizational performance	South Africa	To define the key contributors to organizational performance, with the view to integrating these contributors to provide a systemic view of organizational performance	*South African Business Journal, 38*(4)
Le Roux, L., & Oosthuizen, H. (2009)	The development of an instructional design model as a strategic enabler for sustainable competitive advantage	South Africa	To put forward a training practice (i.e., an instructional design model) that intersects with business-level strategy and aims to improve job-specific knowledge and productive behavior as factors pertinent for achieving sustainable competitive advantage	*South African Business Journal, 41*(1)
Engelbrecht, A. S., Van Aswegen, A. S. et al. (2005)	The effect of ethical values on transformational leadership and ethical climate in organizations	South Africa	To develop and validate a theoretical model to explain the structural relationships between transformational leadership with ethical climate and ethical values in the South African business context	*South African Business Journal, 36*(2)
Poovan, N., Du Toit, M. K. et al. (2006)	The effect of the social values of Ubuntu on team effectiveness	South Africa	Explore the management of South Africa's diverse workforce by analyzing the impact of the social values of Ubuntu on specific characteristics of team effectiveness	*South African Business Journal, 37*(3)
Gaylard, M., Sutherland, M. et al. (2005)	The factors perceived to influence the retention of information technology workers	South Africa	To identify the most important variables for retaining information technology workers	*South African Business Journal, 36*(3)
Anyster, W., Goodman, S. et al. (2006)	The formation of self-efficacy beliefs of skilled professional employees in a South African fruit export organization	South Africa	To explore the formation of self-efficacy beliefs from the perspective of individual employees occupying formal roles within the supply chain division of an international fruit marketing organization	*South African Business Journal, 37*(4)

(continued)

Authors	Title	Country	Purpose	Journal/ Publication
Morrison, J. M., Brown, C. J. et al. (2008)	The impact of organizational culture on project management in matrix organizations	South Africa	To empirically examine the relationship between organizational culture and the effectiveness of project management	*South African Business Journal, 39*(4)
De Klerk, S. (2010)	The importance of networking as management skill	South Africa	To determine the importance of networking as a management skill	*South African Business Journal, 41*(1)
Venter, E., Boshoff, C. et al. (2003)	The influence of relational factors on successful succession on family business: A comparative study of owner managers and successors	South Africa	To identify the relational or human factors that impact successful succession	*South African Business Journal, 34*(4)
Arnolds, C. A., & Boshoff, C. (2004)	The management of the early stages of restructuring in a tertiary education institution—An organizational commitment perspective	South Africa	To investigate the impact of restructuring (mergers) on the organizational commitment, job performance, and intent to resign of tertiary education staff	*South African Business Journal, 35*(2)
Klem, C., & Schlechter, A. F. (2008)	The relationship between leader emotional intelligence and psychological climate: An exploratory study	South Africa	To investigate the relationship between two important constructs for organizations: leader emotional intelligence and psychological climate	*South African Business Journal, 39*(2)
Struwig, F. W., & Smith, E. E. (2002)	The relationship between organizational culture and strategy formulation in South African firms	South Africa	To investigate the relationship between organizational culture and strategy formulation in South African firms	*South African Business Journal, 33*(1)
Oosthuize, H. (2005)	The relationship between strategic process dimensions and organizational output performance—A South African investigation in relation to global best practices	South Africa	To research the understanding and assessment of strategic process behavior in South Africa	*South African Business Journal, 36*(4)

(continued)

Authors	Title	Country	Purpose	Journal/ Publication
Visser, D. J., de Coning, T. J. et al. (2005)	The relationship between the characteristics of the transformational leader and the entrepreneur in South African SMEs	South Africa	To identify the profile elements of entrepreneurship and transformational leadership in SMEs, which, if applied appropriately, will in all probability lead to organizational innovation; and to determine whether entrepreneurs in SMEs in the South African context possess characteristics that manifest them as transformational leaders	*South African Business Journal, 36*(3)
Van Heerden, C. H., & Barter, C. (2008)	The role of culture in the determination of a standardized or localized marketing strategy	South Africa	To explore the possible convergence of global strategy, the way in which culture and marketing affect and are affected by one another, culture's role in the localization or standardization of a marketing strategy, as well as which elements of the marketing strategy to standardize versus localize	*South African Business Journal, 39*(2)
Hugo, P. F., & Loubser, S. S. (2005)	The role of managed healthcare in the South African context—A systemic approach	South Africa	Since managed health care represents a collection of interventions, it is probable that these interventions will provoke responses that either support or counter the objectives of the intervening parties. The study focuses on trends that can be quantified to demonstrate this process, as well as on qualitative responses from role-players within the system to explain behavioral changes that give rise to these trends.	*South African Business Journal, 36*(3)

(continued)

Authors	Title	Country	Purpose	Journal/ Publication
Johnson, G. D. (2009)	The social dimension of multi-racial advertising: Its impact on consumers' attitudes.	South Africa	To investigate whether South African companies, by integrating a multiracial feature in an advertisement, create the perception among consumers that their advertisement is socially responsible and, in so doing, increase their brand equity	*South African Business Journal, 40*(2)
Smith, E. E., & Kruger, J. (2005)	Perceptions of graduates regarding workplace expectations: An exploratory study	Malawi	To outline the results of a study that investigates the perceptions of graduates regarding workplace expectations	*South African Business Journal, 36*(1)
Denner, M., & Oosthuizen, H. (2008)	The strategic positioning and configuration of national mapping organizations as enablers of economic and social growth in South Africa	South Africa	This paper explores the transferability and application of business-driven strategic thinking to that of a public sector context, namely, national mapping organizations.	*South African Business Journal, 36*(3)
Brown, C. J. (1999)	Towards a strategy for project management implementation	South Africa	The basic tenet of this article is that the implementation of project management as a way of managing, in formerly functionally structured organizations, is a complex process requiring strategic management intervention.	*South African Business Journal, 30*(2)
Botha, D. F. (2005)	Towards an instrument for surveying knowledge management practices	South Africa	To develop and stabilize a methodology, including a data collection and analysis instrument, for an annual audit of knowledge management (KM) practices in the SA business sector	*South African Business Journal, 36*(1)

(continued)

Authors	Title	Country	Purpose	Journal/ Publication
Steyn, C., & Kahn, M. (2008)	Towards the development of a knowledge management practices survey for application in knowledge intensive organizations.	South Africa	To explore the theoretical and methodological approach used in the development of a survey aimed at measuring employee perceptions of KMPs within the Human Sciences Research Council (HSRC), one of South Africa's largest public KIOs dedicated to social science research that makes a difference	*South African Business Journal, 39*(1)
Hipkin, I. B. (2000)	TQM: The paradox of empowerment and conformance in the service sector	South Africa	This study describes the implementation of TQM in a South African insurance company that wished to improve quality through empowerment.	*South African Business Journal, 31*(1)
Boshoff, C. (2007)	Understanding service recovery satisfaction from a service encounter perspective: A pilot study	South Africa	To investigate service recovery from a service encounter perspective by considering the influence of what the complaining customer can visually see during the encounter	*South African Business Journal, 38*(2)
Johnston, K. A., Abader, T. et al. (2009)	Understanding the outsourcing decision in South Africa with regard to ICT	South Africa	Information and Communication Technology (ICT) outsourcing is a strategic initiative adopted by many organizations across all industries. The research was performed using a number of statistical tests and descriptive analysis methods to explore the literature and to determine the current status of South Africa's ICT outsourcing market.	*South African Business Journal, 40*(4)
Akande, W. A., & Banai, M. (2009)	Your next boss is American: Attitudes of South African managers towards prospective US-South African joint ventures	South Africa	To explore South African managers' expectations of prospective South African-U.S. international joint ventures	*South African Business Journal, 40*(2)

(continued)

Authors	Title	Country	Purpose	Journal/ Publication
Mbeta, P. (2007)	The effect of national culture on management behavioral norms in Malawi	Malawi	To explore the effect of national culture on management organizational behavior in Malawi	Dissertation (Benedictine University)
Ali, S. et al (2001)	Indigenizing organizational change: Localization in Tanzania and Malawi	Malawi	Takes as a starting point several conclusions, based on a considerable amount of evidence, that a contingency approach to organizational change is required in countries that are developing	*Journal of Managerial Psychology, 16*(1)
Jones, M. L. (1989)	Management development: An African focus	Malawi	To focus on managerial thinking in Malawi and how that can be utilized to coach and train managers	*International Studies of Management & Organization, 19*(1)
Jones, M. (1988)	Managerial thinking: An African perspective	Malawi	Cross-cultural studies of managerial attitudes, beliefs, and values have produced evidence to support both the view that industrialization is a force for convergence and the notion that national cultural realities continue to support divergence. Data from an investigation of Malawian managers are considered in relation to those from comparable previous studies in other countries, and more specifically in terms of the African context.	*Journal of Management Studies, 25*(5)
Carr, S. C. (1995)	Managing motivational gravity in Malawi	Malawi	The term *unidirectional drive upwards* describes the desire of individuals to stand out from and rise above the crowd. Although this desire to rise above others is well documented, little attention has been directed to the social consequences of such achievement.	*Journal of Social Psychology, 135*(5)

(continued)

Authors	Title	Country	Purpose	Journal/ Publication
Carr, S. (1998)	Actors, observers, and attributions for Third World poverty: Contrasting perspectives from Malawi and Australia	Malawi and Australia	To observe attributions for Third World poverty using contrasting perspectives from Malawi and Australia. Any confirmation of the presence of an actor-observer effect in Western observers' attributions for Third World poverty, potentially, could be used to sensitize the donor public to their donor bias.	*Journal of Social Psychology, 138*(2)
De Vreede, G.-J., Jones, N. et al. (1998)	Exploring the application and acceptance of group support systems in Africa	Malawi	Cross-cultural group support systems (GSS) field studies are scarce. Although the state of knowledge and theory development in this area warrants a focus on descriptive field explorations, most cross-cultural GSS research has taken place in laboratory environments. The study reported here represents the first detailed descriptive field study of GSS application in Africa.	*Journal of Management Information Systems, 15*(3)
Chirwa, E. W. (2004)	Industry and firm effects of privatization in Malawian oligopolistic manufacturing	Malawi	To evaluate the impact of privatization on technical efficiency using panel data from privatized enterprises, state-owned enterprises, and private enterprises competing in oligopolistic Malawian manufacturing industries in which privatization took place	*Journal of Industrial Economics, 52*(2)

(continued)

Authors	Title	Country	Purpose	Journal/ Publication
MacLachlan, M., Mapundi, J. et al. (1995)	The acceptability of a Western psychometric instrument in a non-Western society	Malawi	This article tests the Managerial and Professional Profiler (MAPP), a personality questionnaire developed in Great Britain for use in occupational settings, among a group of managers from Malawi. Personality tests are becoming increasingly popular. It is now well recognized that using psychometric instruments developed within one cultural context to assess human attributes in another cultural context is fraught with difficulties. One aspect of psychometric acceptability across cultures that has been largely ignored is face validity. In the very broadest sense, this concept may refer to whether the instrument appears acceptable to respondents in terms of what it sets out to achieve.	*Journal of Social Psychology, 135*(5)
Kalanda, B. K. (1997)	Developing a quality culture for Malawian industries: A case study of the Malawi Bureau of Standards	Malawi	To develop a quality culture for Malawian industries	*Total Quality Management, 8*(2/3)

(continued)

Authors	Title	Country	Purpose	Journal/ Publication
Botha, D. (2005)	Towards an instrument for surveying knowledge management practices	Malawi and South Africa	To create an understanding of the differences in the preferences of cultural styles toward knowledge processes and thus of knowledge management initiatives in multinational organizations. An understanding of this nature could contribute to a change in the way that existing knowledge management initiatives are applied within the context of international organizations. This would greatly enhance and improve the effectiveness and efficiency of knowledge management initiatives on a global scale.	*South African Journal of Business Management, 36*(1)
Bolden, R., & Kirk, P. (2009)	African leadership. Le leadership Africain: L'apparition de nouvelles facultas de compransion grÃ¢ce au daveloppement du leadership	Malawi and South Africa	To provide an account of meanings and connotations of "African leadership" emerging from research with a cohort of participants on a pan-African leadership development program	*International Journal of Cross Cultural Management, 9*(1)
Prinsloo, E. D. (2000)	The African view of participatory business management	Malawi and South Africa	To delineate the group of activities concerned with business and then proceed to give an exposition of the concepts used by Ubuntu as an example of the African view of business management indicating those activities of human performances regarded by them as basic to their world view	*Journal of Business Ethics, 25*(4)

(continued)

Authors	Title	Country	Purpose	Journal/ Publication
Stivers, E. (1989)	An American visitor in South Africa: Analysis of authority-subordinate relations between Whites and Blacks	South Africa	The study analyzed 10 South African situations encountered on a 3-week professional and sightseeing visit. The group that conducted the study consisted of American psychologists. They examined each setting in terms of factors that separated Blacks and Whites into positions of authority and subordination.	*Organization Development Journal, 7*(3)
Du Toit, Louw (1987)	Leadership for the future: A large system OD intervention in South Africa	South Africa	This case study is only a synopsis of an OD project that was born out of a desperate need to contribute toward peaceful and constructive change in South Africa.	*Organization Development Journal, 5*(2), 46–52
Preston, J., Du Toit, L., Van Zyl, D. A., & Holscher, F. (1993)	Team building in South Africa: Cross cultural synergy in action	South Africa	This case study discusses the endemic nature of violence in South Africa. The authors describe two educational interventions that followed this model.	*Public Administration Quarterly, 15*(1), 65–82
Gorelick, C., & April, K. A. (2004)	BP case study: KM team structuration and sense-making	South Africa	The 3-year case study was designed to learn how a virtual project team contributed to organizationwide learning, with specific interest in two dimensions: structuring and sensemaking.	*South African Journal of Business Management, 35*(1), 1–16
Grutter, Field, Faull, & Norman (2002)	Work team performance over time: Three case studies of South African manufacturers	South Africa	A case study of a South African manufacturing firm that made significant efforts to implement shop floor improvement teams	*Journal of Operations Management,* (20), 641–657

(continued)

Authors	Title	Country	Purpose	Journal/ Publication
Fauconnier & Marthur-Helm (2008)	Black economic empowerment in the South African mining industry: A case study of Exxaro Limited	South Africa	This case study explores some key challenges and opportunities in the implementation of the broad-based Black empowerment deal of Kumba Resources, which subsequently led to the formation of Exxaro Limited, a large Black-owned mining conglomerate in South Africa.	*South African Journal of Business Management, 39*(4), 1–14
Van Wyk, Bowen, & Akintoye (2008)	Project risk management practice: The case of a South African utility company	South Africa	This case study documents the risk management practice of a utility company for its Recovery Plan project to address the risks of power interruptions due to a shortfall of supply and increasing electricity demand.	*International Journal of Project Management, 26*(2), 149–163
Byrne & Sahay (2007)	Participatory design for social development: A South African case study on community-based health information systems	South Africa	In this case study, the role of participation within the domains of information system (IS) research and social development is analyzed. The case study involved the design and development of a community-based health IS in a rural area of South Africa.	*Information Technology for Development, 13*(1), 71–94
Dovey, K. (2002)	Leadership development in a South African health service	South Africa	To present the outcomes of the work-based methodology aimed at the development of leadership capacity in district health management teams in the East Cape province of South Africa; concept of work-based learning; details on the case study of a work-based learning partnership in the South African state health sector; development of transformational leadership capacity	*International Journal of Public Sector Management, 15*(7), 520

(continued)

Authors	Title	Country	Purpose	Journal/ Publication
Reddy, Moodley, & Maharajj (2000)	Human resources capacity-building in local government	South Africa	The case study is about the Training and Development Scheme (TDS), an affirmative action-based program located in the Greater Durban area of Kwazulu-Natal. The TDS was one of the mechanisms utilized to address the underrepresentation of Black (Indian, Colored, and African) employees in management of public institutions.	*Public Personnel Management, 29*(2), 293
Travis, R., McFarlin, N., Van Rooyen, C. A. J., & Gray, M. (1999)	Community development in South Africa: Its use as an intervention strategy	South Africa	To explore whether community development was an appropriate intervention strategy to address the lack of resources in the communities of Cato Crest, Bhambayi, and Ndwedwe from the perspective of three major role-players or stakeholders in community development	*International Social Work, 42*(2), 177–187
Preston, J., & Armstrong, T. (1991)	Team building in South Africa: Cross cultural synergy in action	South Africa	To discuss the idea of cultural synergy in team building and the development of cultural synergy throughout the stages of consultation, when the authors attended a two-and-a-half-day meeting of the Community Development and Management Association of Africa	*Public Administration Quarterly, 15*(1)
Smith, K. K., Miller, R. S. & Kaminstein, D. S. (2003)	Consultant as container: Assisting organizational rebirth in Mandela's South Africa	South Africa	This case study recounts an intervention into the senior leadership group of a state-owned organization in South Africa.	*Journal of Applied Behavioral Science, 39*(2)
Morris, M., Bessant, J., & Barnes, J. (2006)	Using learning networks to enable industrial development: Case studies from South Africa	South Africa	To explore the dynamics of interfirm learning and the ways in which "learning networks" can be established and facilitated.	*International Journal of Operations & Production Management, 26*(5)

(continued)

Authors	Title	Country	Purpose	Journal/ Publication
Moholo, B., Thomas, L., & Taylor, J. (2000)	Urban NGOs in transition: The case of Johannesburg, South Africa	South Africa	The process of urbanization in Johannesburg recently has taken place within the context of a transition from Apartheid rule to democracy. South African NGOs, once recognized as a key element of civil society in the fight against Apartheid, have been forced to reinvent themselves in order to justify continued funding.	*Occasional Paper series, 23*(1)
Kamfer, Louw-Potgieter, & Boy (1991)	Organizational bridge building through stereotype reduction	South Africa	The development of an organizational Intergroup Intervention in the form of a stereotype reduction workshop is described. Based on an effective American model, it had to be adapted for the South African situation and its theoretical base consciously reformulated. Some early outcomes are also discussed.	Academy of Management Best Papers Proceedings
Yachkaschi, S. (2005)	Capacity building at the grassroots: Piloting organizational development of community based organizations in South Africa	South Africa	To explore the use of OD for capacity building of community-based organizations (CBOs) in South Africa. The author works for Community Connections, a South African nonprofit support organization that predominantly provides support to CBOs and community workers. In 2004, the organization initiated an OD pilot program.	INTRAC Praxis Note, No. 18
Symes, C. (2006)	Mentoring leaders of HIV/AIDS community based organizations: Reflecting on the Barnabas Trust's approach in South Africa	South Africa	To describe an innovative mentoring approach to leadership development that simultaneously builds the capacity of the CBO as an organization. This approach is being pioneered by the Barnabas Trust in South Africa, which works alongside 53 HIV and AIDS-related CBOs.	INTRAC Praxis Note, No. 24, 1–11

(continued)

Authors	Title	Country	Purpose	Journal/ Publication
World Bank (2003)	Capitalizing on local knowledge—Community knowledge exchange: Case Study: Rooibos Tea and community-based tourism knowledge exchange	Malawi	Establishment of new tourism initiatives, training, and capacity building for tourism businesses, production, and marketing of traditional crafts. Farmer organization: structures and cooperation for small-scale farmers at a community level, communal tea-making facilities.	World Bank
UNAIDS (2002)	The faces, voices, and skills behind the GIPA workplace model in South Africa: UNAIDS case study	South Africa	A pilot program, the GIPA Workplace Model, has been developed over the past 4 years with the support of the United Nations Development Program (UNDP) and the World Health Organization (WHO). Its aim was to place trained fieldworkers, living openly with HIV/AIDS, in selected partner organizations in different sectors so that they could set up, review, or enrich workplace policies and programs.	UNAIDS
World Bank (2003)	Capitalizing on local knowledge—Mbongolwana knowledge exchange with Lake Chilwa communities	Malawi	The Mbongolwana Wetland Management Project was established 2 years ago to address the problems of degradation. It promotes improved management of the wetlands and is managed by a steering committee of local community-based structures and support agencies from the government, NGOs, and private sectors.	World Bank
Nunns, C. G., & Bluen, S. D. (1992)	The impact of behavior modeling training on self-reports of White supervisors in two South African mines	South Africa	The present study assessed whether behavior modeling training would improve the self-reports of White, first-line supervisors in relation to their Black subordinates in two South African mines. Self-reports of behavior were elicited from 50 supervisors equally split into experimental and control groups.	*Journal of Applied Behavioral Science, 28*(3)

(continued)

Authors	Title	Country	Purpose	Journal/ Publication
Lynham, S. A. & Cunningham, P. W. (2004)	Human resource development: The South African case	South Africa	Faced by the challenges of the past and by pressure to become increasingly competitive internationally, South Africa has recognized that the education, training, and development of its labor force and citizenry will be instrumental to its long-term economic growth and social well-being. Consequently, an integrated framework of policy and legislation is being implemented to ensure that human resource development is firmly placed on the national agenda.	*Advances in Developing Human Resources, 6*(3)
Cunningham, P. W. Lynham, S. A. & Weatherly, G. (2006)	National human resource development in transitioning societies in the developing world: South Africa	South Africa	As a developing country in the past decade, South Africa has undergone a significant transformation in its national human resource development framework.	*Advances in Developing Human Resources, 8*(1)
Digoamaje, M. (2004)	Reorganization of libraries under greater Johannesburg in the Democratic Era	South Africa	In the last 10 years of democracy, the country has experienced major changes. There was no way that libraries could escape these changes. This paper looks at the journey undertaken by the City of Johannesburg Library Services, from the time they were under the administration of nine local governments to date, where they are now under the City of Johannesburg Administration.	LIASA 2004 Conference, Limpopo

(continued)

Authors	Title	Country	Purpose	Journal/ Publication
English, J. (2002)	Managing cultural differences to improve industrial efficiency	South Africa	The route to changing perceptions is through training supported by qualitative and quantitative feedback and assessment. Employees of a major construction company followed an in-house training program comprising theoretical input on groups, management, and culture, and experiential exercises based on the philosophy of Ubuntu.	*Building Research & Information, 30*(3)
James, R., & CABUNGO staff (2009)	Faith based organization development (OD) with churches in Malawi	Malawi	This paper is based on practical OD consultancy experiences of CABUNGO and INTRAC with more than 20 church-based organizations in Malawi between 2000 and 2006. It analyzes the common and particular organizational challenges that church-based organizations face and explores what should be different about OD with such organizations. Complementary research was carried out with Islamic FBOs (faith-based organizations) in Malawi, published as Praxis Note 48, "Capacity Building with Islamic FBOs."	INTRAC Praxis Note, 47
Perkins, R., Lockee, B., & Burton, J. (2005)	Building human capacity in Malawi: Contextual considerations in industrial technology project implementation	Malawi	In its effort to provide the country of Malawi with quality education programs, USAID sponsors a program that links U.S.-based institutions of higher learning with Malawian institutions. This is a capacity-building case of human resources and institutional capacity.	Education Media and Technology Year Book, 30

(continued)

Authors	Title	Country	Purpose	Journal/ Publication
Kaaria, Njuki, Abenakyo, Delve, & Sanginga (2008)	Assessment of the enabling rural innovation (ERI) approach: Case studies from Malawi and Uganda	Malawi	This paper presents lessons from applying an innovative action research approach for linking smallholder farmers to markets in eastern and southern Africa. The Enabling Rural Innovation (ERI) approach aims to strengthen social organization and entrepreneurial capacity in rural communities. It focuses on fostering community-based capacity for the inclusion of rural women and the poor in analyzing and accessing market opportunities.	*Natural Resources Forum, 32*(1)
McGill, R. (1993)	Institution building for a Third World city council: Some lessons from the practice	Malawi	In January 1989, the Overseas Development Administration (ODA) started a 3-year institution-building project for Malawi's three city councils. Discusses how it became apparent in Lilongwe that the project's traditional notions of institution building were limited and how its concern was for financial and general efficiency, while its environment—the city—was ignored.	*International Journal of Public Sector Management, 6*(5)
Tambulasi, R. (2007)	Decentralization opening a new window for corruption: An accountability assessment of Malawi's four years of democratic local governance	Malawi	This article evaluates the first 4 years of decentralized local governance in Malawi with special focus on accountability of local assemblies. The article mainly relies on primary sources such as newspapers, governmental and nongovernmental reports, and a comparative literature survey.	*Journal of Asian and African Studies, 42*(2)

(continued)

Authors	Title	Country	Purpose	Journal/ Publication
Satali, L. (2008)	Informal organic responses to HIV/AIDS in the workplace: An action research focusing on Malawian civil societies	Malawi	HIV policies are a vital tool in helping CSOs (civil society organizations) respond to HIV and AIDS in the workplace. But because they are the most easily measured response, there is a danger that they will become the only way to gauge whether a CSO is responding. When we focus too much on workplace policy, it makes organizations feel under pressure from donors to develop policy as a funding hoop. They do not own the policy development process, so they do not implement it later.	*CABUNGO,* 1–9
Chibwana, B., & Mohan, P. (2001)	The role of information, education and communication in the Malawi social action fund	Malawi	The Malawi Social Action Fund (MASAF) began implementation in 1996 and is now midway through the second phase (MASAF 2). Before MASAF, the country's experience with self-help projects and programs had not been notably successful. MASAF was designed to improve the record by promoting a change in the way all development actors—including, and perhaps especially, the government—would work with other stakeholders.	*Human Development Network, 1*(3)
James, R. (2002)	What makes CSO coalitions effective? Lessons from Malawi	Malawi	The last few years have witnessed a seismic shift in the perceived role of civil society. Donors in particular have recognized that "more pluralistic forms of governance and decision-making are seen to be more effective in developing a social consensus about structural changes in the economy and other key reforms."	INTRAC_Occasional Paper Series, 38

(continued)

Authors	Title	Country	Purpose	Journal/ Publication
James, R. (2003)	Leaders changing inside out: What causes leaders to change behavior? Cases from Malawi Civil Society	Malawi	Our experience of capacity building has shown that for organizations to fundamentally change, their leaders themselves have to change. Leadership development is universally recognized as a priority capacity-building need for strengthening civil society in Africa. Yet our knowledge of how and why this critical process occurs is quite limited. To address this gap, INTRAC undertook a 50-day research project in Malawi to understand more about this process of change among civil society leaders.	INTRAC Occasional Paper Series, 43
Rode, H. (2005)	Capacity building in an AIDS-affected health care institution	Malawi	It is increasingly clear that capacity building for those civil society organizations (CSOs) working in contexts of high HIV/AIDS prevalence presents specific challenges and costs. However, there have been few documented experiences that explore these challenges and costs and suggest ways to address them appropriately. This Praxis Note is an attempt to fill that gap. It will initially provide an overview of the impacts of HIV/AIDS on the Malawi health care system and on the organizational capacity of Mulanje Mission Hospital (MMH).	INTRAC Praxis Note, 11

(continued)

Authors	Title	Country	Purpose	Journal/ Publication
James, R & CABUNGO (2005)	Building capacity to mainstream HIV/AIDS internally: Reflecting on CABUNGO's experience with NGOs in Malawi	Malawi	The consultants observed that much of the gender work with NGOs in Malawi to date had concentrated on training and failed to bring about the hoped for organizational change. As supposed specialists in organizational development and change, they felt challenged to make a difference.	INTRAC Praxis Note, 13
James, R. (2005)	Creating space for greed	Malawi	To present a spiritual approach to OD consultancy in Malawi	*INTRAC*, 1–3
Saddiq, N. (2009)	Capacity building and Islamic FBOs: Insights from Malawi	Malawi	Islamic FBOs are not well understood. Until recently, they have been largely ignored in the development discourse. But they are now playing a significant role in development. If external stakeholders are to engage productively with Islamic FBOs, they need to develop their understanding and appreciation of them.	INTRAC Praxis Note, 48, 1–9
James, R. (2005)	Vision quest: Learning about leadership development in Malawi	Malawi	The context in which most civil society organizations (CSOs) work is constantly evolving, often rapidly. In response, leaders of CSOs must therefore be leaders of change in their own organizations. In order for organizations to develop and change, practical capacity-building experiences are revealing that leaders themselves have to develop and change.	INTRAC Praxis Note, 17

(continued)

Authors	Title	Country	Purpose	Journal/ Publication
Wrigley, R. (2006)	Learning from capacity building practice: Adapting the most significant change approach to evaluate capacity building provision by CABUNGO in Malawi	Malawi	This paper provides a reflection on a pilot experience of using the Most Significant Change (MSC) methodology to evaluate the capacity-building services of CABUNGO, a local capacity-building support provider in Malawi. MSC is a story-based, qualitative, and participatory approach to monitoring and evaluation (M&E). INTRAC and CABUNGO worked collaboratively to adapt and implement the MSC approach to capture the complex and often intangible change resulting from capacity building, as well as to enhance CABUNGO's learning and performance.	INTRAC Praxis Paper, No. 12
Kaaria, S., Njuki, J. et al. (2008)	Assessment of the enabling rural innovation (ERI) approach: Case studies from Malawi and Uganda	Malawi	This study presents lessons from applying an innovative action research approach for linking smallholder farmers to markets in eastern and southern Africa.	*Natural Resources Forum, 32*(1),
Malunga, C. (2003)	An investigation into the factors affecting staff turnover amongst professional staff in NGOs in Malawi	Malawi	The role of OD in curbing professional staff turnover in a Malawian nongovernmental organization called the Youth Development Organization.	Unpublished Master of Arts Thesis, University of South Africa
Malunga, C. (2007)	Improving the effectiveness of strategic planning in local NGOs in Malawi	Malawi	An investigation into the effectiveness of strategic planning processes in a Malawian NGO called the Center for Youths and Children Affairs (CEYCA), Human Rights Resource Center (MHRRC), Malawi Network of People Living with HIV and AIDS (MANET), Active Youths in Social Enhancement(AYISE).	Unpublished Doctor of Literature and Philosophy Dissertation, University of South Africa

(continued)

Authors	Title	Country	Purpose	Journal/ Publication
CORAT	From anger to laughter	Malawi	An intervention that involved resolving anger issues between an international NGO and a local church in Malawi. The consultant goes through the OD process, utilized for the church, to agree to develop a strategic plan that would release it from the partnership with the international NGO.	http://developingchurches.ning.com/page/case-studies
Sulamoyo, D. (2010)	I am because we are: Ubuntu as a cultural strategy for OD and change in sub-Saharan Africa	Malawi and South Africa	The article explores the concept of Ubuntu as a cultural philosophy and way of life in Africa that has an influence on OD strategies for change and development.	*Organization Development Journal, 28*(4)
Murrell, K. (1986)	Africa and organization development: Is there any chance?	Africa	International development and OD are natural partners, and the combination may well provide new ideas and insights into the ways in which development work can occur on a global basis. It is the author's position that OD has much to gain in testing itself in the developing world as well as introducing a process of change that has more cultural adaptability and local control than the traditional expert model of developing country assistance.	*Organization Development Journal, 4*(1)
Najafbagy, R. (1990)	Culture and development in Third World countries	Third World countries	Understanding a particular culture requires a correct comprehension of its underlying ideas and intelligent appreciation of its aesthetic forms. It is, however, the values of a culture that contain its essence and offer the best way to understand it and participate in it.	*Organization Development Journal, 8*(4)

(continued)

Authors	Title	Country	Purpose	Journal/ Publication
Handford, J. S., & L. D. Coetsee (2003)	Essential transformational leadership skills to mobilize people: Combating Africa pessimism, the South African leadership challenge	South Africa	South Africa has seen many challenges since the historical first democratic election in 1994. The post-Mandela era is characterized by an abundance of so-called transformational plans but an inability of some political leader, government officials, and other leaders to convert the majority of these plans into actions. Probably the most important underlying problem is a lack of transformational leadership skills. This paper identifies three crucial transformation leadership characteristics, which are critical for leaders to introduce change and mobilize people to manage change effectively.	*Organization Development Journal, 21*(1)
Armstrong, T. R. (1989)	Experiencing large systems change in South Africa	South Africa	This is a report on a South African experience and the changes of perspective the author went through as he tried to comprehend and help those with whom he worked. He was convinced that as they tried to be facilitators of change, they, as the consultants, would be changed too. To be effective facilitators of large systems change, they need to be brave enough to seek out solutions where none existed.	*Organization Development Journal,* (Fall)

(continued)

Authors	Title	Country	Purpose	Journal/ Publication
Moore, C. T. (1990)	Non-violent change in South Africa: Comments by three organization directors	South Africa	This article is based on a visit by the author to South Africa in December 1988/January 1989. During this time, several interviews were held with people active in a variety of social, educational, business, and political organizations. The common element in all three organizations is the concern with nonviolent solutions to the political, social, and economic situations in South Africa. The potential implications for external OD intervention are discussed.	*Organization Development Journal,* (Winter)
Njoku, P. C. (1992)	Non violent large systems change: Developing an international agenda for non violent solutions	Africa	With increasing turbulence in the world, the idea of extending the practices of organizational development to national and international conflicts may provide a tempting route to world peace. OD must help to create new world organization policies whereby humanity can better handle its urgent problems. Ideas leading to a less violent world, rather than trying to create a nonviolent world, may be the correct path to take.	*Organization Development Journal, 10*(2)
Van der Merwe, H. W., Meyer, G., & Honikman, K. (1989)	Political mediation in South Africa: Some problems and challenges	South Africa	Mediators in South Africa are faced by serious obstacles, including the great asymmetry of power between the establishment and opposition groups, and the problems of prevailing violence. These problems largely account for the scarcity of mediating bodies in South Africa and highlighted the need for training in negotiating and mediating skills.	*Organization Development Journal,* (Fall)

(continued)

Authors	Title	Country	Purpose	Journal/ Publication
Rogers, C., & Sanford, R. (1986)	Reflections on our South African experience	South Africa	Carl Rogers and Rush Sanford completed a 7-week stay in South Africa, where they worked with Blacks and Whites in an attempt to achieve a peaceful, tranquil existence. Employing person-centered therapy, they attempted to create a psychological climate where all divergent feelings could be openly expressed and nonjudgmentally accepted.	*Organization Development Journal,* (Winter)
Scott, D. (1992)	The organization as a vehicle for social change: South Africa . . . An opportunity	South Africa	South Africa is located at a critical point on the globe, where both First and Third Worlds have to meet. This article aims to give perspective on how organizations can be a powerful vehicle for social change and to suggest tentative steps for a continued productive approach tempered with realism.	*Organization Development Journal, 10*(3)
Ogaba Otokpa, A. E. (1992)	The dynamics of social pollution and organizational development in Africa	South Africa	Complex technology greatly affects business today. Success in African organization development demands organizational teamwork and sound management principles. New OD technology is creating revolutionary changes both in and outside the organization. This paper looks at the widespread alienation and apathy of many people toward business and the establishment and suggests how OD can better serve them.	*Organization Development Journal, 10*(1)

(continued)

Authors	Title	Country	Purpose	Journal/ Publication
Reese, V. P. (1989)	A systems approach to viewing South Africa	South Africa	This paper viewed the historical origins of the present problems with Apartheid in South Africa. It offered a generalized view of the observations of the author as a member of the Organization Development Institute research study team and the reframed specific observations from the perspective of group systems behavior. The theories used were from intergenerational family therapy.	
LEKGOTLA (2002)	Report of the public-private interactions Lekogtla	South Africa	Public-Private health sector Interactions (PPI) are on the increase in South Africa. However, there are few mechanisms for the two sectors to routinely engage with each other. The PPI Lekgotla was a follow-up to the discussions on PPIs initiated at the National Health Summit held in November 2001. The Lekgotla was seen as one step in an ongoing process of strengthening the relationship and communication between the public and private health sectors.	
Department of Justice (2008)	Review of the Western Cape Strategic Action Plan (MTSF) 2007/2008	South Africa	The need for this review emanates from the strategic direction set by the Minister and EXCO at the National Lekgotla in December 2005. The result of the National EXCO Lekgotla was the Department's Medium Term Strategic Framework (MTSF) policy document, which directs all our service delivery objectives and Action Plan for the Western Cape.	Department of Justice

(continued)

Authors	Title	Country	Purpose	Journal/ Publication
Thomas, A. L., & Bendixen, M. (2000)	The management implications of ethnicity in South Africa	South Africa	This study is on the management of ethnicity in South Africa. Key to managing cultural diversity in the workplace is the promotion of management effectiveness in an inclusive organizational culture. South Africa has a long history of exotic peoples settling in the region. These influxes have created considerable conflict between the various exotic groups and between the exotic and indigenous populations, especially as the colony expanded into the areas occupied by the indigenous peoples. Given the history of conflict and ethnic diversity, it seems unlikely that South Africa would have a common national culture.	*Journal of International Business Studies, 31*(3)
Jackson, T., & Kotze, E. (2005)	Management and change in the South African National Defense Force: A cross-cultural study	South Africa	The military in South Africa has gone through major changes as part of the wider society's transition from Apartheid to democracy, necessitating the integration of a multicultural force This article develops a theoretical framework for understanding these cross-cultural dynamics. It reports an empirical management study investigating the perceptions of the different cultural groups to better understand the process of cross-cultural integration in an institution whose stability and success has major implications for Southern African society. It finds significant differences in attitudes among cultural groups. This has implications for understanding multicultural change processes in similar institutions in transition around the world.	*Administration & Society, 37*(2)

Malawian Tables From Meta-Analysis

TABLE A.2 Types of OD Interventions Within Settings for Malawi

Individual Applications Classified by Setting

	For-Profit		Not-for-Profit		Public		Community	
Type of OD Intervention Malawi	**No.**	**%**	**No.**	**%**	**No.**	**%**	**No.**	**%**
Diagnostic Activities	0	0%	3	13%	0	0%	0	0%
Process Analysis Activities	0	0%	1	4%	0	0%	0	0%
System-Building Activities	0	0%	1	4%	0	0%	0	0%
Team-Building Activities	0	0%	0	0%	0	0%	0	0%
Intergroup Activities	0	0%	3	13%	0	0%	0	0%
Technostructural Activities	0	0%	3	13%	2	100%	1	50%
Skill-Building Activities	0	0%	5	22%	0	0%	1	50%
Coaching/Counseling Activities	0	0%	1	4%	0	0%	0	0%
Strategic Planning Activities	0	0%	6	26%	0	0%	0	0%
Total	**0**	**0%**	**23**	**100%**	**2**	**100%**	**2**	**100%**

TABLE A.3 Totals for Types of OD Interventions for Malawi

Individual Applications Classified by Setting—Malawi

Type of OD Intervention	**No.**	**%**
Diagnostic Activities	3	11%
Process-Analysis Activities	1	4%
System-Building Activities	1	4%
Team-Building Activities	0	0%
Intergroup Activities	3	11%
Technostructural Activities	6	22%
Skill-Building Activities	6	22%
Coaching/Counseling Activities	1	4%
Strategic Planning Activities	6	22%
Total	**27**	**100%**

TABLE A.4 Types of OD Interventions Within System Levels for Malawi

Individual Applications Classified by System

	Individual		Group		Organization	
Type of OD Intervention Malawi	**No.**	**%**	**No.**	**%**	**No.**	**%**
Diagnostic Activities	0	0%	1	20%	2	11%
Process-Analysis Activities	0	0%	0	0%	1	5%
System-Building Activities	0	0%	0	0%	1	5%
Team-Building Activities	0	0%	0	0%	0	0%
Intergroup Activities	0	0%	1	20%	2	11%
Technostructural Activities	0	0%	1	20%	5	26%
Skill-Building Activities	3	100%	2	40%	1	5%
Coaching/Counseling Activities	0	0%	0	0%	1	5%
Strategic Planning Activities	0	0%	0	0%	6	32%
Total	**3**	**100%**	**5**	**100%**	**19**	**100%**

TABLE A.5 Rating Factors Within System Levels for Malawi

Individual Applications Classified by System and Degree of Effects

	Individual		Group		Organization	
Rating Factor Malawi	**No.**	**%**	**No.**	**%**	**No.**	**%**
Highly positive and intended effects	1	33%	2	40%	7	37%
Definite balance of positive and intended effects	1	33%	1	20%	7	37%
No appreciable effects	1	34%	1	20%	3	16%
Negative effects	0	0%	1	20%	2	10%
Total	**3**	**100%**	**5**	**100%**	**19**	**100%**

TABLE A.6 Combined Rating Factors for Malawi Within System Levels Out of Total Number of Interventions

Individual Applications Classified by Success

	Success		No Success		Total	
System Level	**No.**	**%**	**No.**	**%**	**No.**	**%**
Group	3	11%	2	8%	5	19%
Individual	2	8%	1	4%	3	12%
Organizational	14	51%	5	18%	19	69%
Total	**19**	**70%**	**8**	**30%**	**27**	**100%**

TABLE A.7 Rating Factors for Malawi

Individual Applications Classified by System—Malawi

Rating Factor	No.	%
Highly positive and intended effects	10	37%
Definite balance of positive and intended effects	9	33%
No appreciable effects	5	19%
Negative effects	3	11%
Total	**27**	**100%**

TABLE A.8 Rating Factors Within Settings for Malawi

Individual Applications Classified by Setting and Degree of Effects

	For-profit		Not-for-profit		Public		Community	
Rating Factor Malawi	**No.**	**%**	**No.**	**%**	**No.**	**%**	**No.**	**%**
Highly positive and intended effects	0	0%	9	39%	0	0%	1	50%
Definite balance of positive and intended effects	0	0%	7	30%	1	50%	1	50%
No appreciable effects	0	0%	5	22%	0	0%	0	0%
Negative effects	0	0%	2	9%	1	50%	0	0%
Total	**0**	**0%**	**23**	**100%**	**2**	**100%**	**2**	**100%**

TABLE A.9 Combined Rating Factors for Malawi Within Settings

Individual Applications Classified by Success

	Success		No Success		Total	
Setting	**No.**	**%**	**No.**	**%**	**No.**	**%**
Community	2	100%	0	0%	2	100%
For-profit	0	0%	0	0%	0	0%
Not-for-profit	16	69%	7	31%	23	100%
Public	1	50%	1	50%	2	100%

TABLE A.10 Types of OD With Rating Factors for Malawi

	Rating Factors							
	Highly Positive and Intended Effects		Definite Balance of Positive and Intended Effects		No Appreciable Effects		Negative Effects	
Type of OD—Malawi	**No.**	**%**	**No.**	**%**	**No.**	**%**	**No.**	**%**
Diagnostic Activities	1	10%	0	0%	0	0%	2	67%
Process-Analysis Activities	1	10%	0	0%	0	0%	0	0%
System-Building Activities	0	0%	1	11%	0	0%	0	0%
Team-Building Activities	0	0%	0	0%	0	0%	0	0%
Intergroup Activities	0	0%	1	11%	2	40%	0	0%
Technostructural Activities	2	20%	2	22%	1	20%	1	33%
Skill-Building Activities	2	20%	3	33%	1	20%	0	0%
Coaching/Counseling Activities	0	0%	1	11%	0	0%	0	0%
Strategic Planning Activities	4	40%	1	11%	1	20%	0	0%
Total	**10**	**100%**	**9**	**100%**	**5**	**100%**	**3**	**100%**

TABLE A.11 Combined Rating Factors for Malawi

Individual Applications Classified by Success

	Success		No Success	
Type of OD Intervention	**No.**	**%**	**No.**	**%**
Diagnostic Activities	1	5%	2	24%
Process-Analysis Activities	1	5%	0	0%
System-Building Activities	1	5%	0	0%
Team-Building Activities	0	0%	0	0%
Intergroup Activities	1	5%	2	24%
Technostructural Activities	4	21%	2	24%
Skill-Building Activities	5	27%	1	14%
Coaching/Counseling Activities	1	5%	0	0%
Strategic Planning Activities	5	27%	1	14%
Total	**19**	**100%**	**8**	**100%**

TABLE A.12 Combined Rating Factors for Malawi Out of Total Number of Interventions

Individual Applications Classified by Success

	Success		No Success		Total	
Type of OD Intervention	**No.**	**%**	**No.**	**%**	**No.**	**%**
Diagnostic Activities	1	4%	2	7%	3	11%
Process-Analysis Activities	1	4%	0	0%	1	4%
System-Building Activities	1	4%	0	0%	1	4%
Team-Building Activities	0	0%	0	0%	0	0%
Intergroup Activities	1	4%	2	7%	3	11%
Technostructural Activities	4	13%	2	7%	6	20%
Skill-Building Activities	5	19%	1	4%	6	23%
Coaching/Counseling Activities	1	4%	0	0%	1	4%
Strategic Planning Activities	5	19%	1	4%	6	23%
Total	**19**	**71%**	**8**	**29%**	**27**	**100%**

About the Author

Dalitso Samson Sulamoyo was born in 1970 in Lilongwe, Malawi, to a Malawian father and Zimbabwean mother. He attended primary school in Malawi and high school in Zimbabwe so that he would have exposure to both parents' cultures. He graduated from Illinois College (Magna Cum Laude) with a BA in Political Science and International Relations. Sulamoyo received a graduate certificate in Public Sector Labor Relations and master's degrees in Political Studies and Public Administration with a focus on nonprofit management from the University of Illinois at Springfield. Sulamoyo holds a PhD in Organization Development from Benedictine University.

Sulamoyo has been the president and CEO of the Illinois Association of Community Action Agencies, a membership organization of 40 not-for-profits and public entities that serve communities and the economically challenged citizens of Illinois for the last 11 years. He also serves as an adjunct faculty member at Benedictine University. He has extensive experience consulting with community action agencies and other organizations in the areas of organization development, change management, capacity building, strategic planning, and leadership development.

Sulamoyo's work has been published in books and leading scholarly journals on the subjects of global organization development, capacity building, and change management. He has presented both nationally and internationally on his work of facilitating change within mission-driven organizations and the understanding of African culture within the context of organization development.

Creating Opportunities for Change and OD in Southern Africa, page 179

Printed and bound by CPI Group (UK) Ltd, Croydon, CR0 4YY

15/09/2026

14962368-0002